FIRST 50 JAZZ STANDARDS

YOU SHOULD PLAY ON THE PIANO

T0087266

ISBN 978-1-4950-7454-7

7777 W. BLUEMOUND RD. P.O. BOX 13819 MILWAUKEE, WI 53213

Visit Hal Leonard Online at
www.halleonard.com

ALONE TOGETHER

Lyrics by HOWARD DIETZ
Music by ARTHUR SCHWARTZ

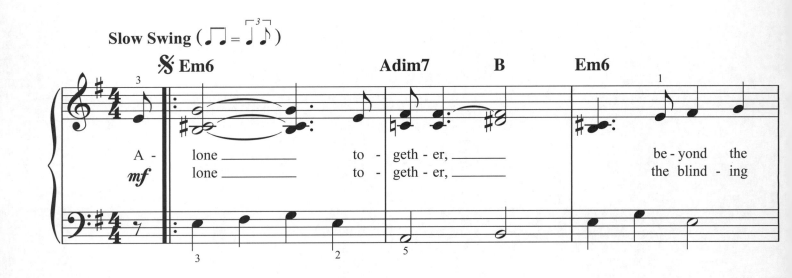

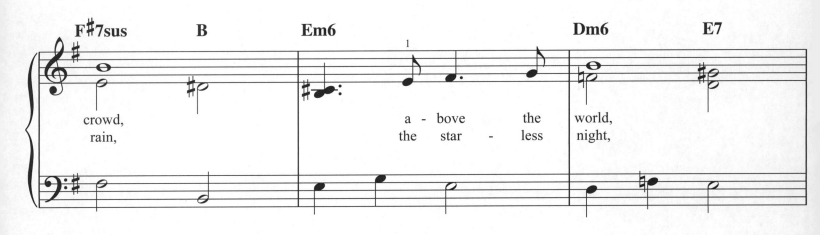

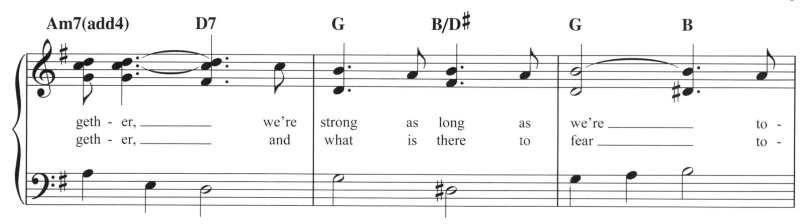

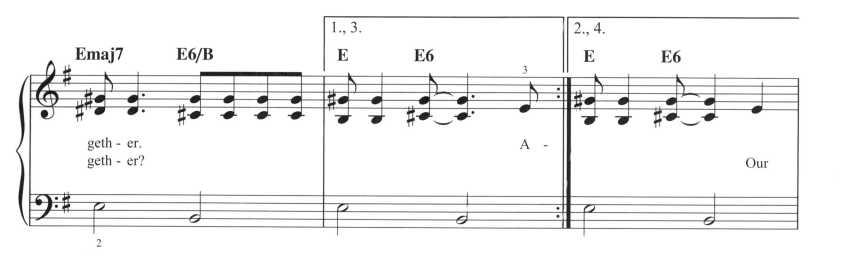

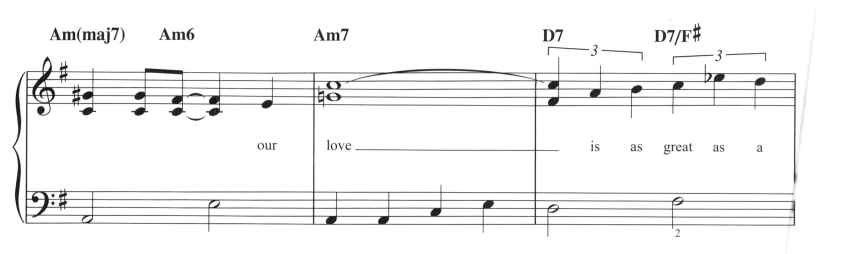

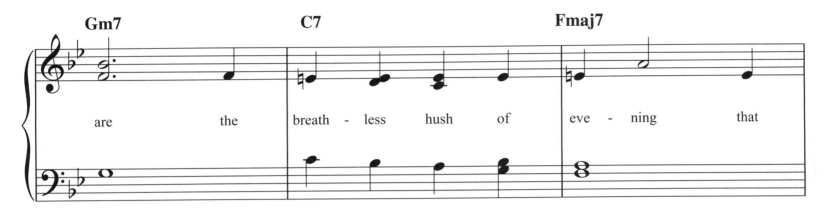

are the breath - less hush of eve - ning that

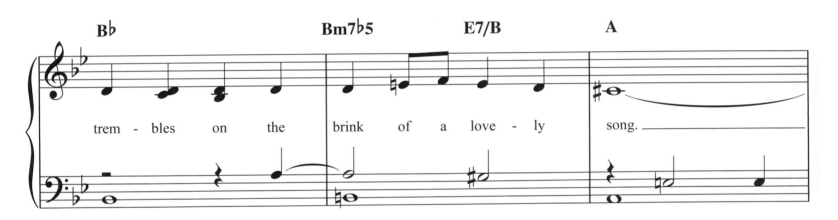

trem - bles on the brink of a love - ly song. ___

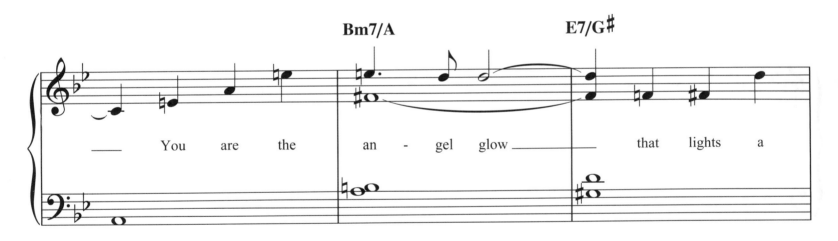

___ You are the an - gel glow ___ that lights a

star, ___ the dear - est things I know ___

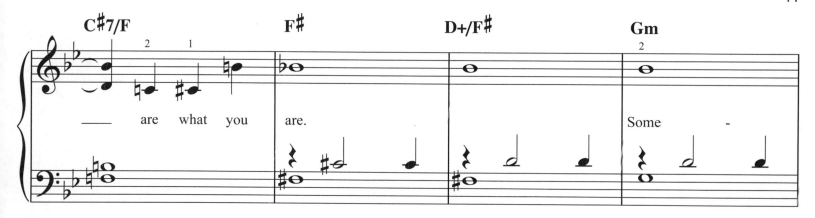

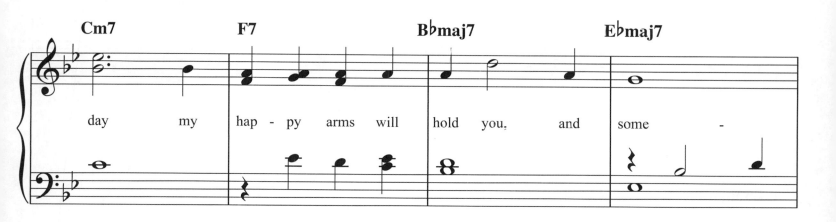

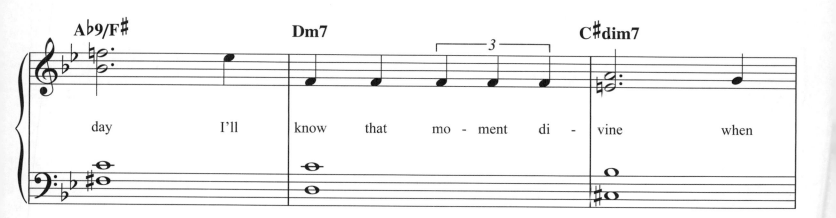

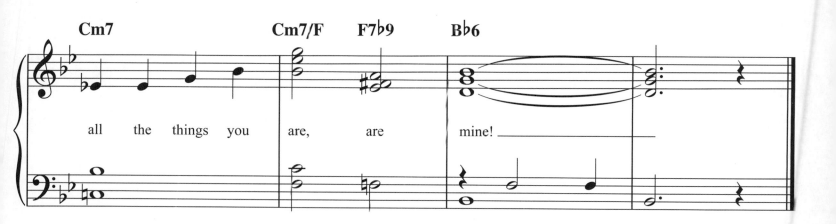

AUTUMN IN NEW YORK

Words and Music by
VERNON DUKE

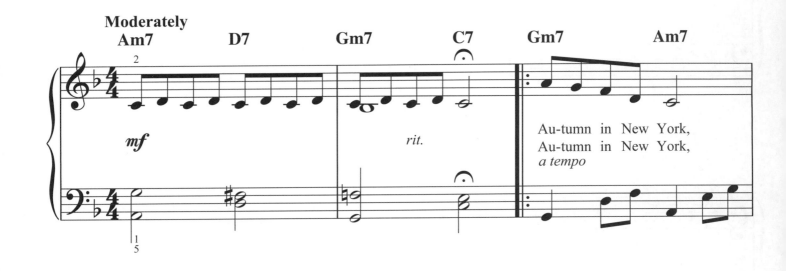

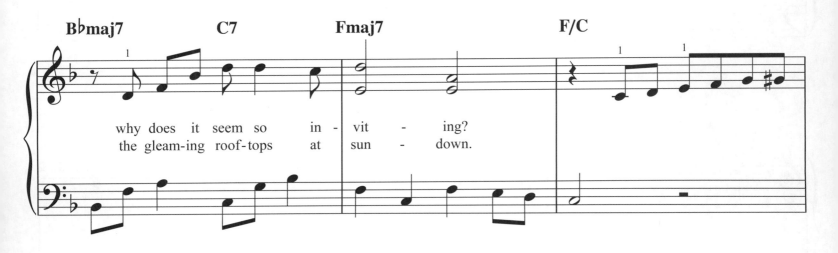

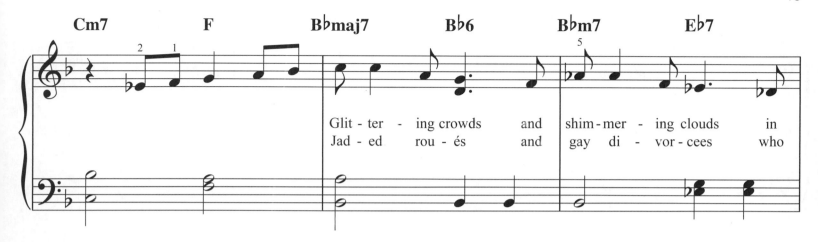

Glit - ter - ing crowds and shim - mer - ing clouds in
Jad - ed rou - és and gay di - vor - cees who

can - yons of steel, they're mak - ing me feel ____ I'm
lunch at the Ritz, will tell you that "it's ____ di -

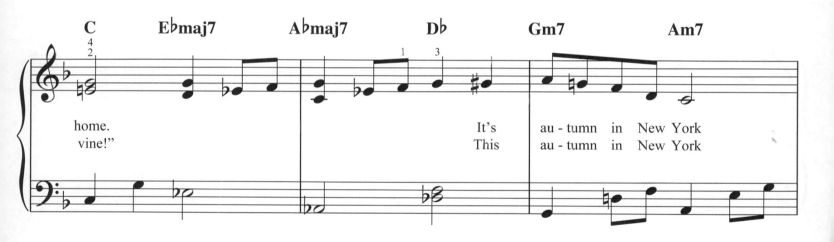

home. It's au - tumn in New York
vine!" This au - tumn in New York

that brings the prom - ise of new love;
trans - forms the slums in - to May - fair;

14

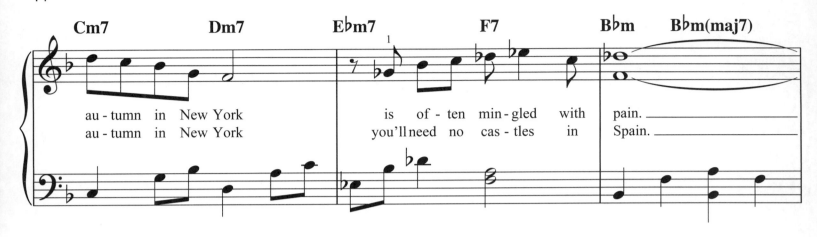

au-tumn in New York
au-tumn in New York

is of-ten min-gled with pain.
you'll need no cas-tles in Spain.

Dream-ers with emp - ty hands may sigh for ex - o - tic
Lov - ers that bless the dark on bench-es in Cen - tral

lands; it's au-tumn in New York, it's good to live it a -
Park greet au-tumn in New York; it's good to live it a -

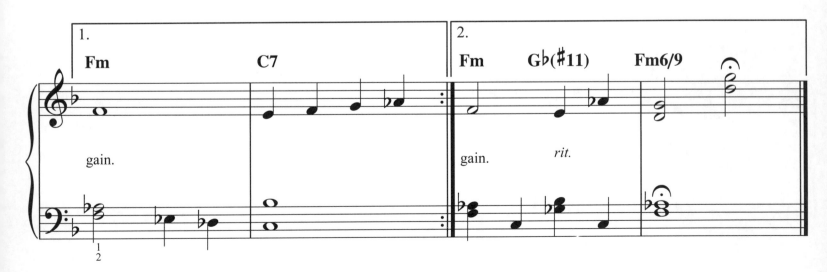

gain.

gain. *rit.*

BODY AND SOUL

from THREE'S A CROWD

Words by EDWARD HEYMAN,
ROBERT SOUR and FRANK EYTON
Music by JOHN GREEN

16

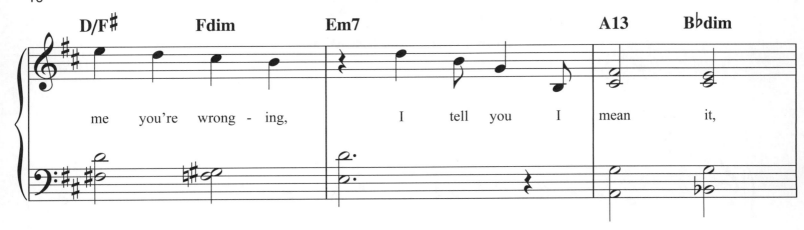

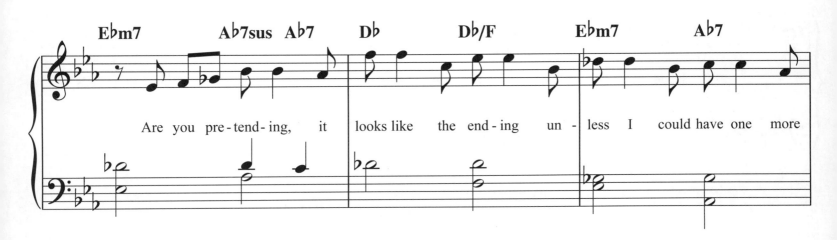

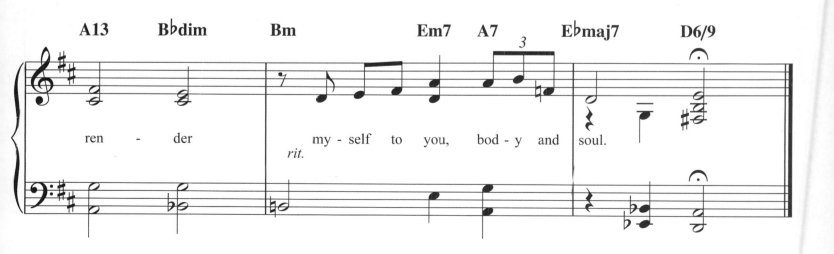

AUTUMN LEAVES

English lyric by JOHNNY MERCER
French lyric by JACQUES PREVERT
Music by JOSEPH KOSMA

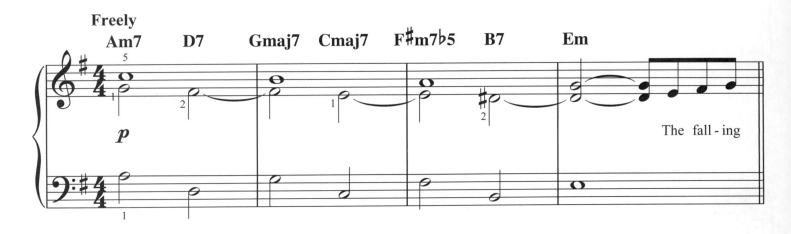

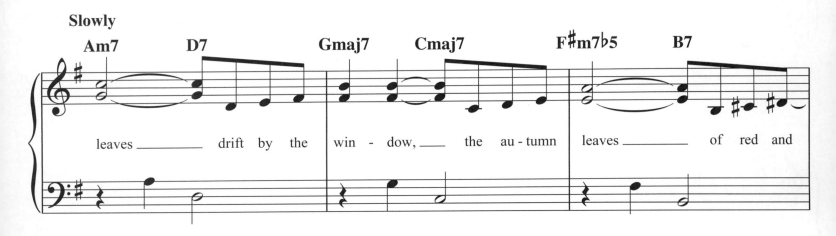

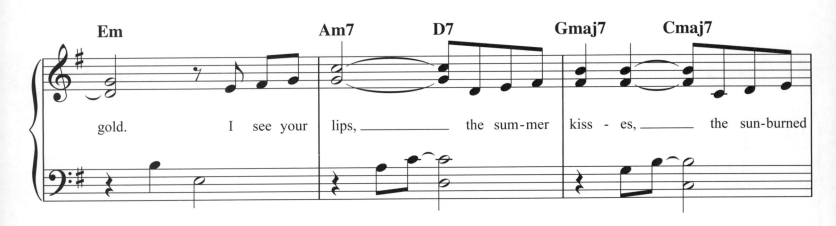

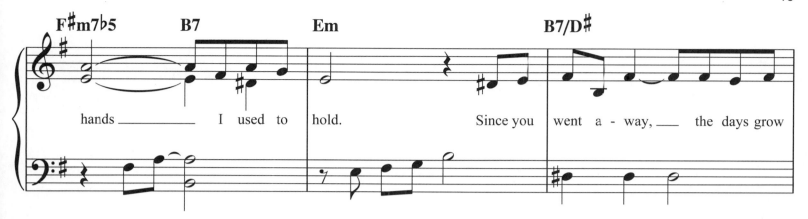

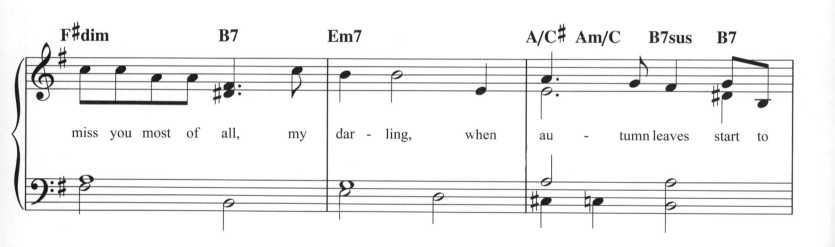

BUT NOT FOR ME

from GIRL CRAZY

Music and Lyrics by GEORGE GERSHWIN
and IRA GERSHWIN

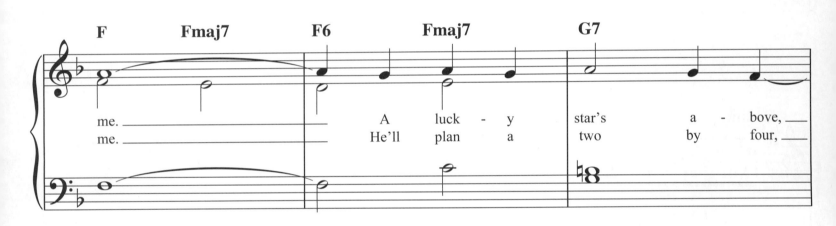

21

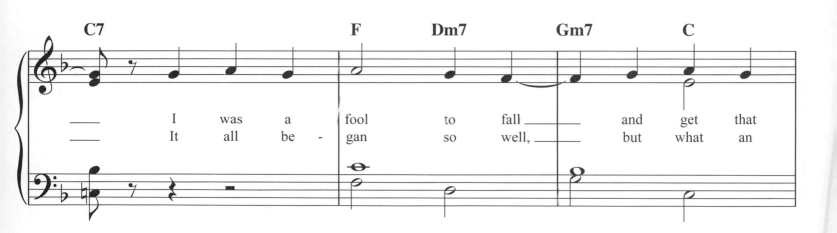

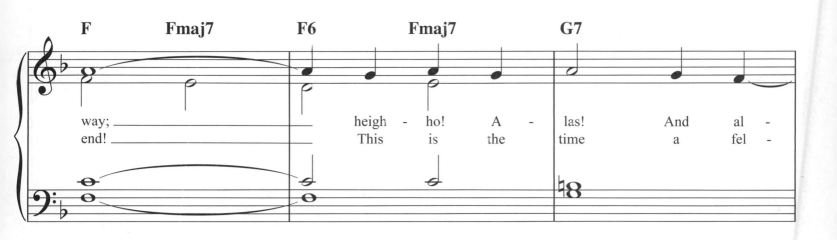

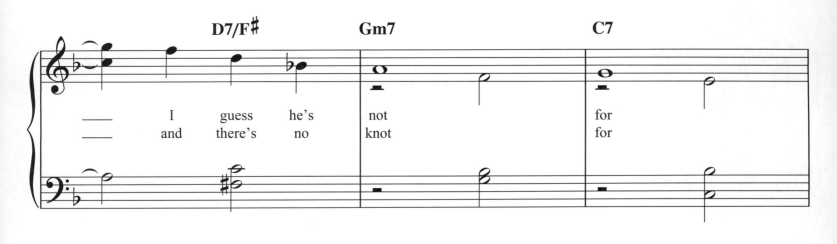

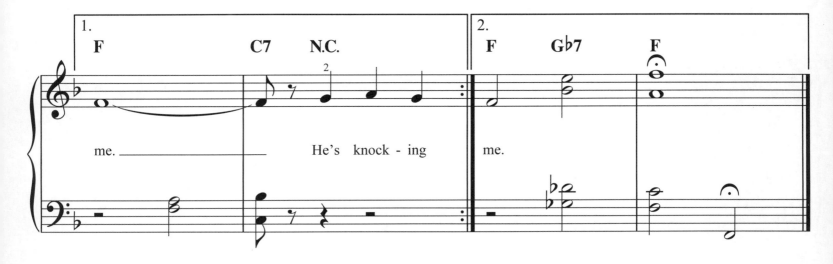

DAYS OF WINE AND ROSES

from DAYS OF WINE AND ROSES

Lyrics by JOHNNY MERCER
Music by HENRY MANCINI

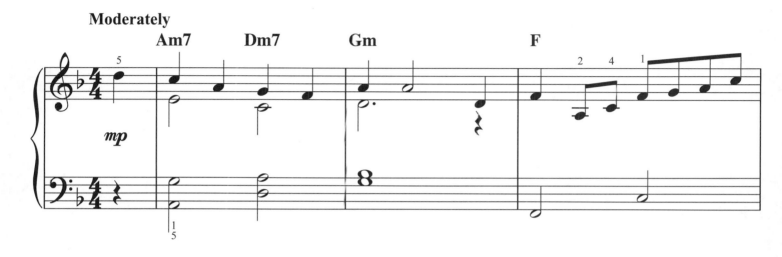

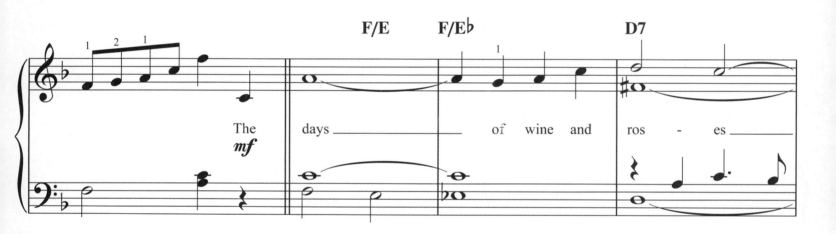

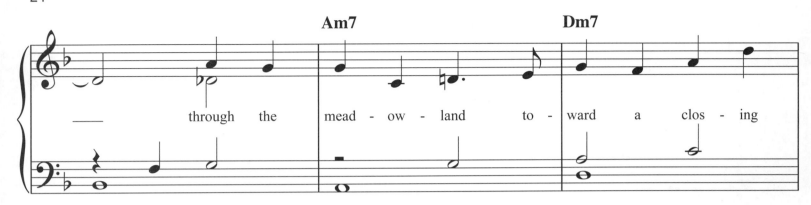

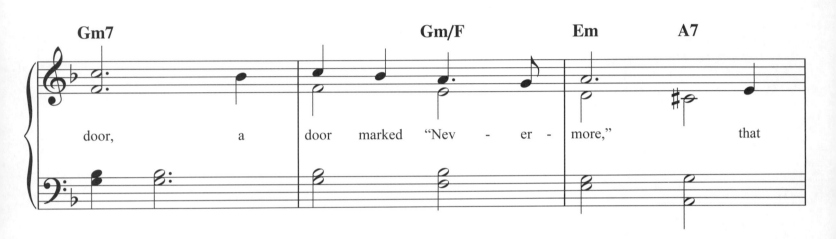

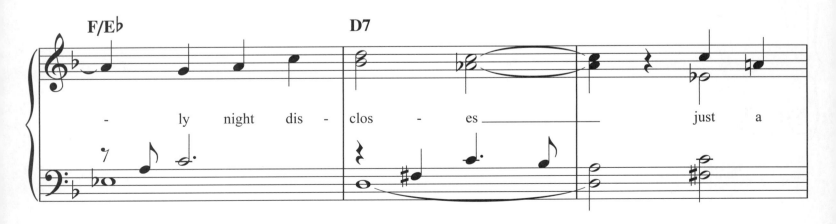

passing breeze   filled with mem - o - ries

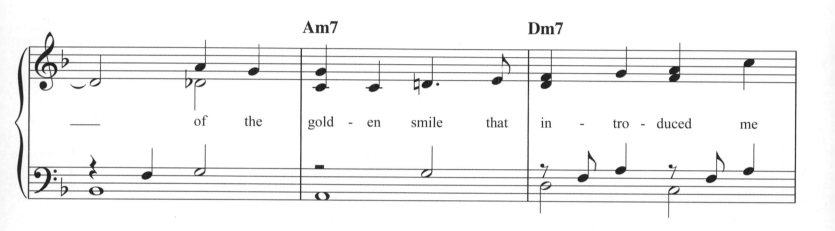

of the gold - en smile that in - tro - duced me

to the days of wine and

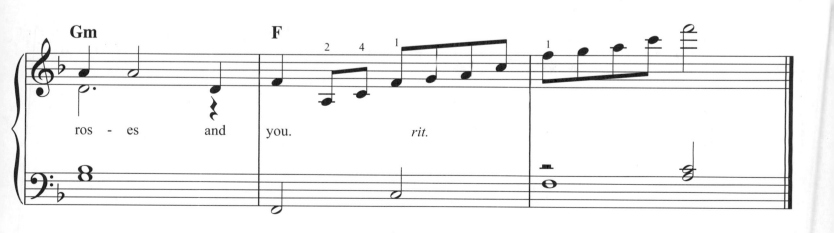

ros - es and you. *rit.*

DON'T GET AROUND MUCH ANYMORE

Words and Music by DUKE ELLINGTON
and BOB RUSSELL

club. Got as far as the door.

D7　　　　　　G7

They'd have ask'd me a - bout you, ___ don't get a - round much an - y -

C　　　　　　　　F6　　　Bb9

more. Dar - ling, I guess my

C(add9)　　　C7　　　F6　　　F#dim

mind's more at ease, ___ but nev - er - the - less,

why stir up mem - o - ries? Been in - vit - ed on dates.

Might have gone but what for? Aw - f'lly dif - f'rent with -

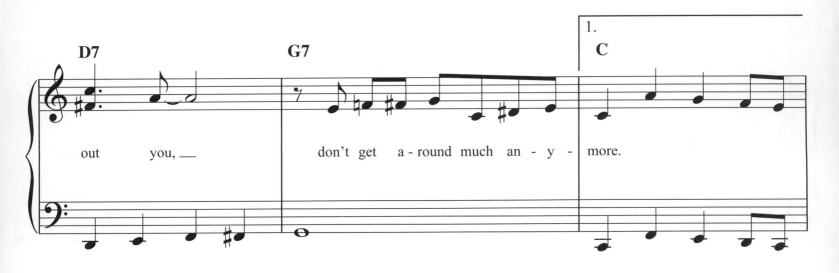

out you, ___ don't get a - round much an - y - more.

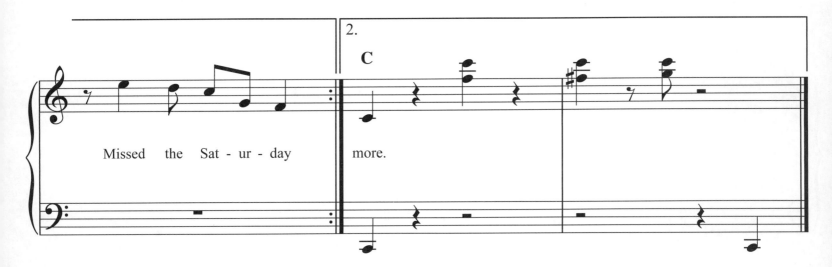

Missed the Sat - ur - day more.

EASY LIVING

Theme from the Paramount Picture EASY LIVING

Words and Music by LEO ROBIN
and RALPH RAINGER

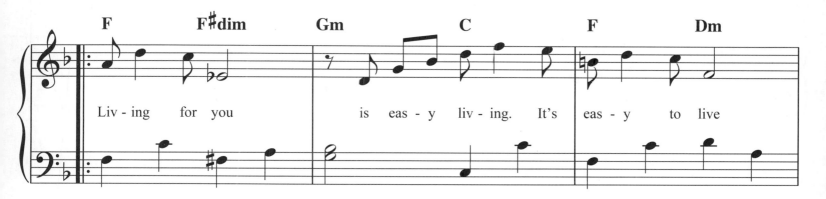

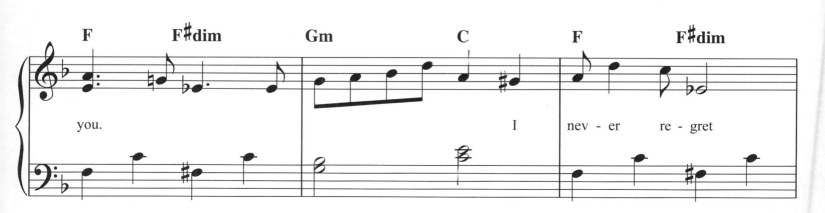

the years I'm giv - ing. They're eas - y to give when you're in love. I'm

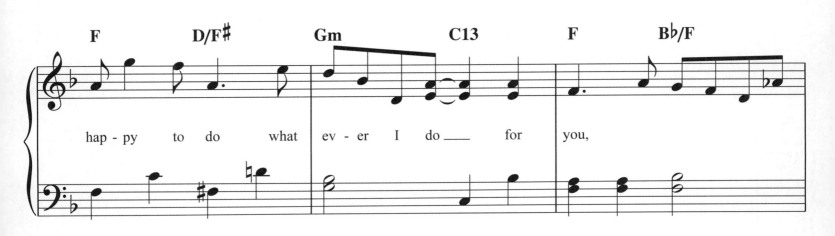

hap - py to do what ev - er I do ____ for you,

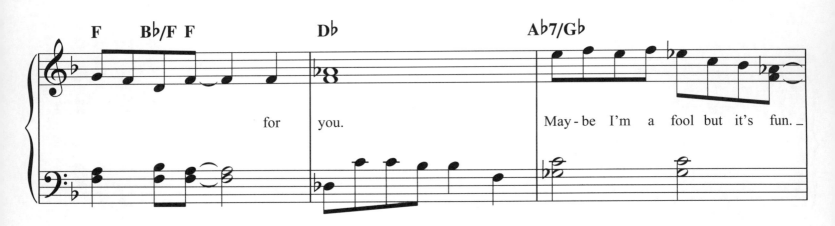

for you. May - be I'm a fool but it's fun. _

____ Peo - ple say you rule me with one ____ wave of your hand. _

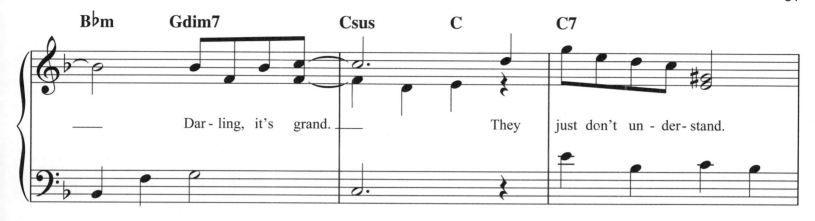

Dar - ling, it's grand. ____ They just don't un - der - stand.

Liv - ing for you is eas - y liv - ing. It's eas - y to live

when you're in love, and I'm so in love, there's noth - ing in life ____ but

1.

you.

2.

you.

FLY ME TO THE MOON
(In Other Words)

Words and Music by
BART HOWARD

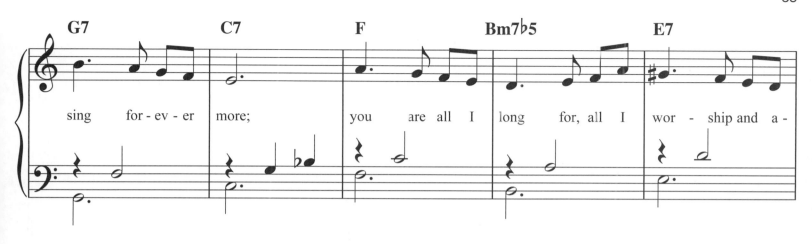

sing for - ev - er more; you are all I long for, all I wor - ship and a -

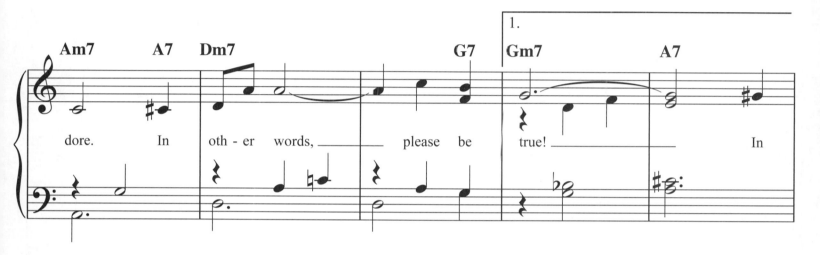

dore. In oth - er words, please be true! In

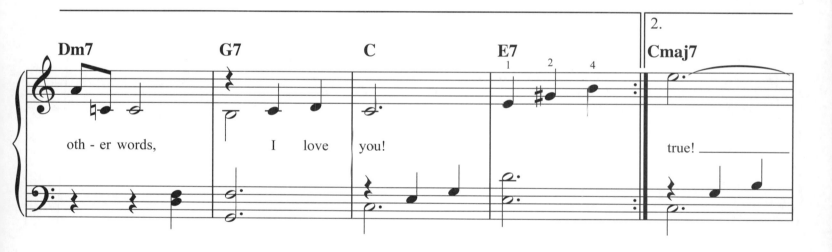

oth - er words, I love you! true!

In oth - er words, I love you!

A FOGGY DAY
(In London Town)
from A DAMSEL IN DISTRESS

Music and Lyrics by GEORGE GERSHWIN
and IRA GERSHWIN

Freely, with motion

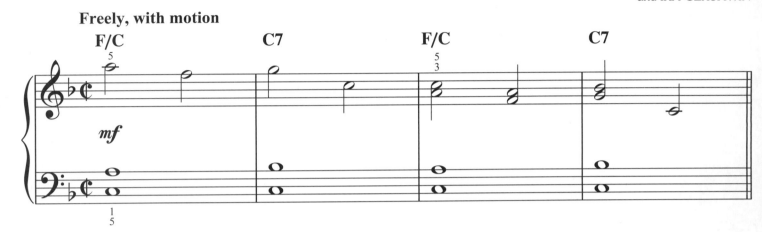

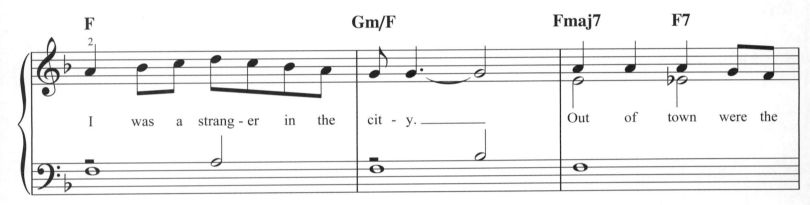

I was a strang-er in the cit-y. ___ Out of town were the

peo-ple I knew. I had a feel-ing of self- pit-y, ___ what to

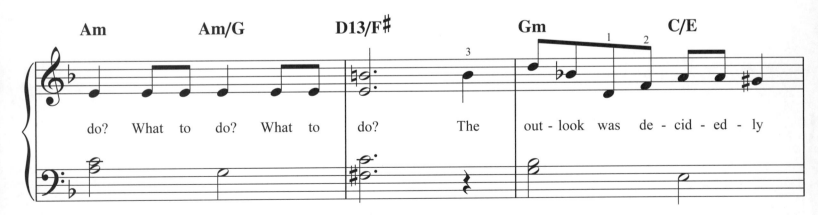

do? What to do? What to do? The out-look was de-cid-ed-ly

blue. _____ But as I walked through the fog - gy streets a - lone, it

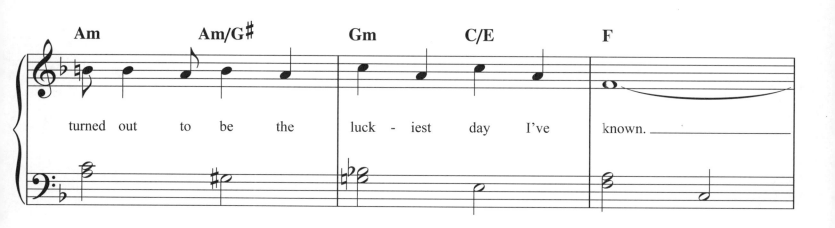

turned out to be the luck - iest day I've known. _____

Moderately fast

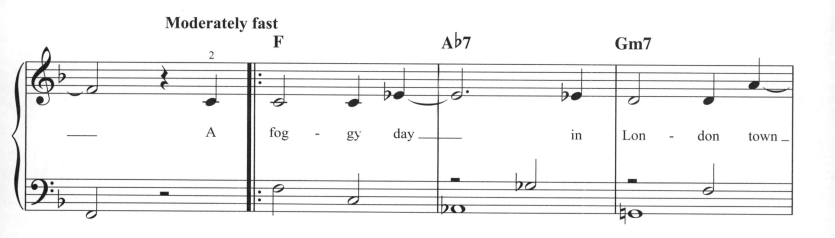

_____ A fog - gy day _____ in Lon - don town _____

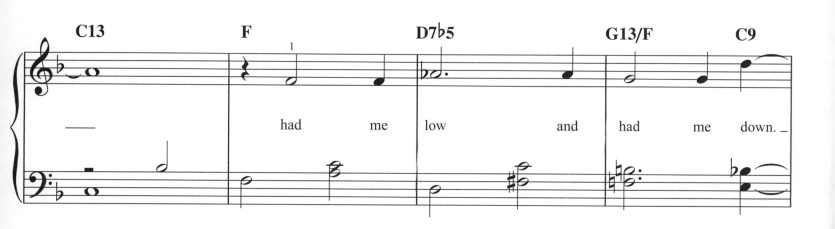

_____ had me low and had me down. _____

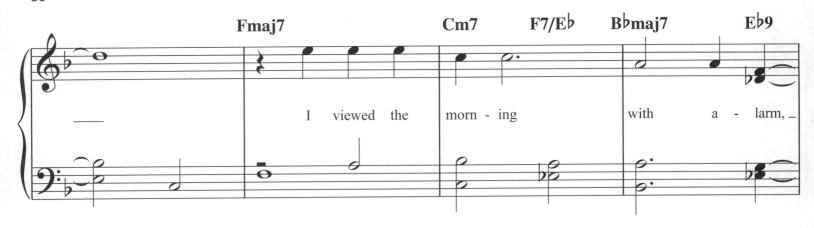

I viewed the morn-ing with a-larm,_

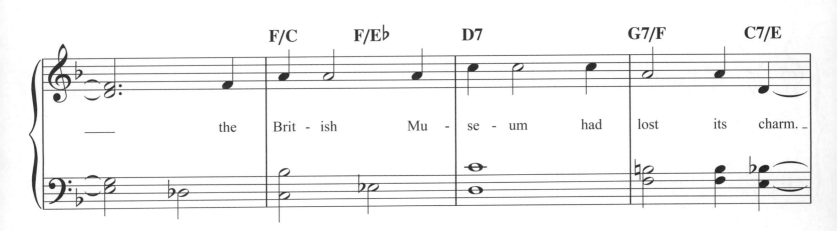

_ the Brit-ish Mu-se-um had lost its charm._

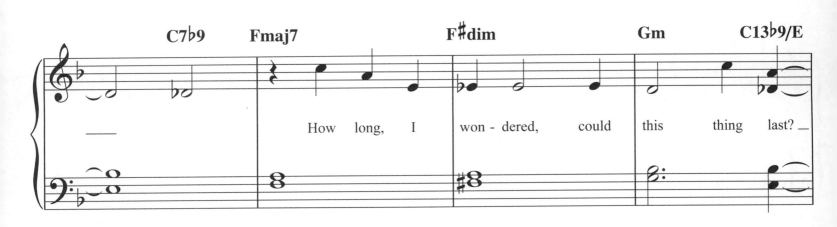

_ How long, I won-dered, could this thing last?_

_ But the age of mir - a - cles had-n't passed,_

37

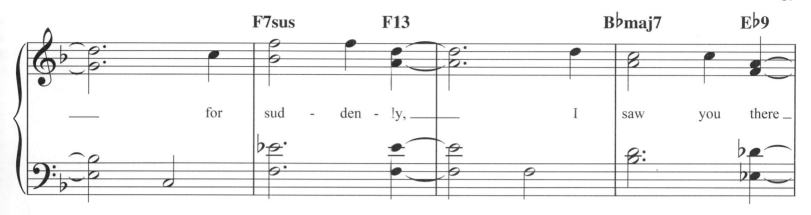

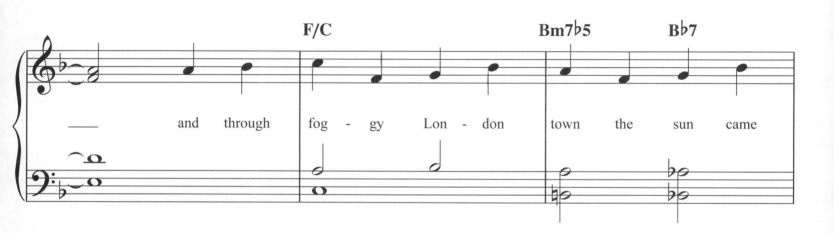

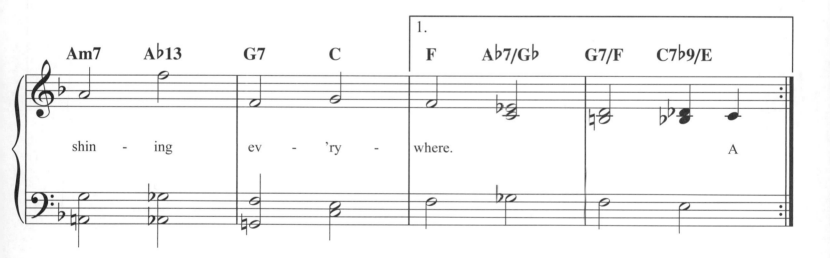

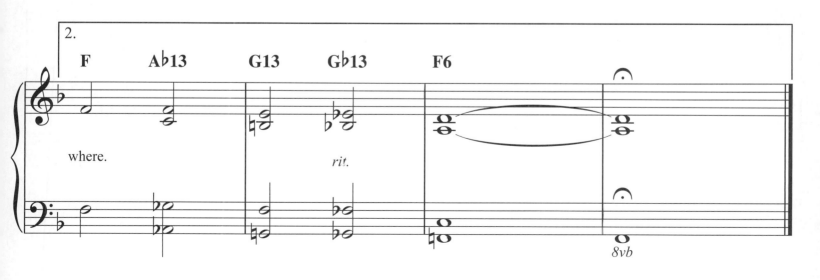

GEORGIA ON MY MIND

Words by STUART GORRELL
Music by HOAGY CARMICHAEL

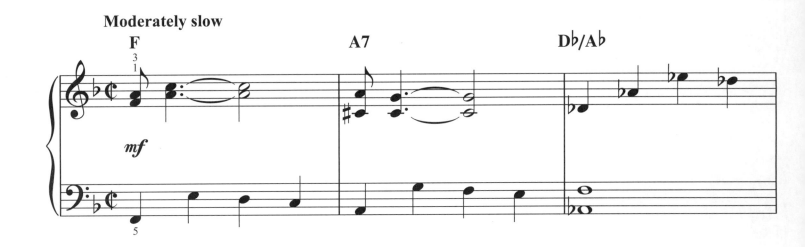

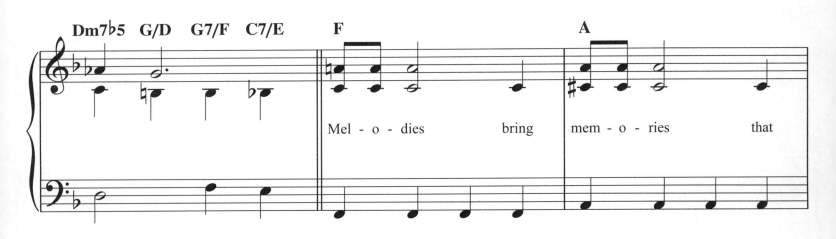

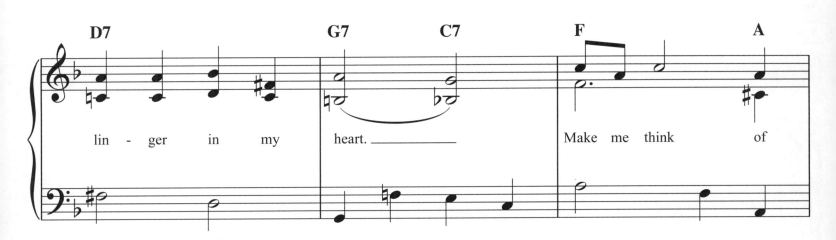

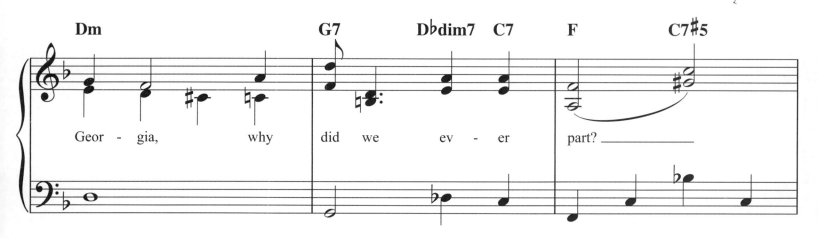

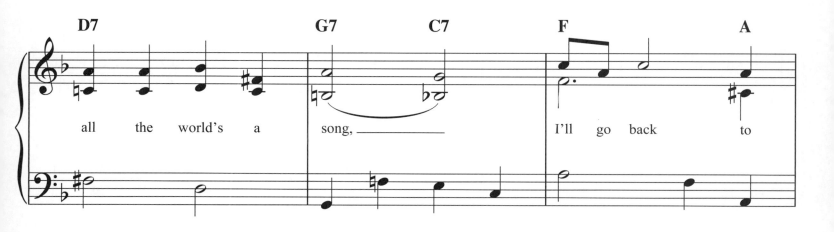

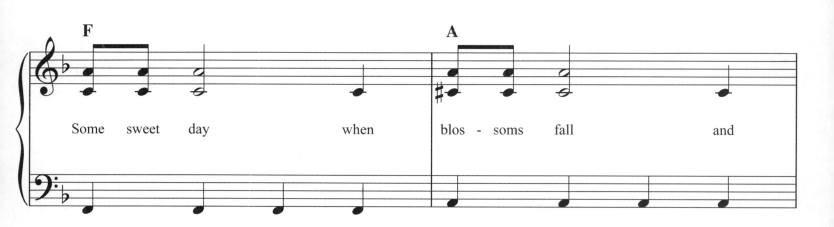

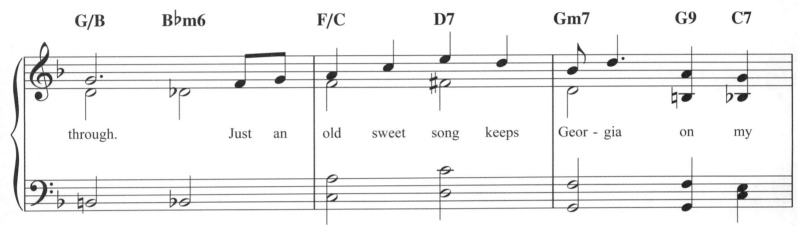

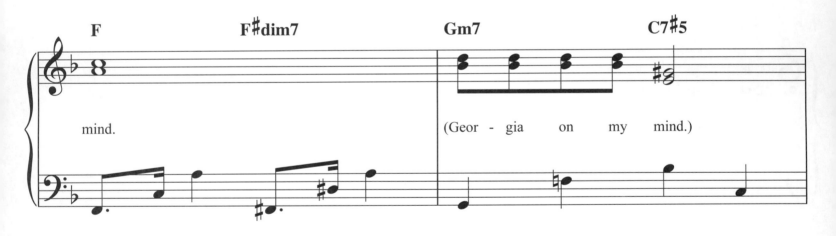

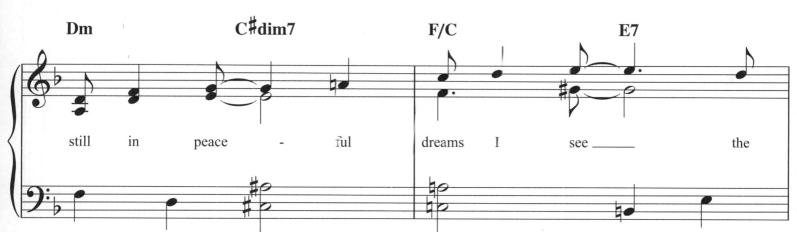

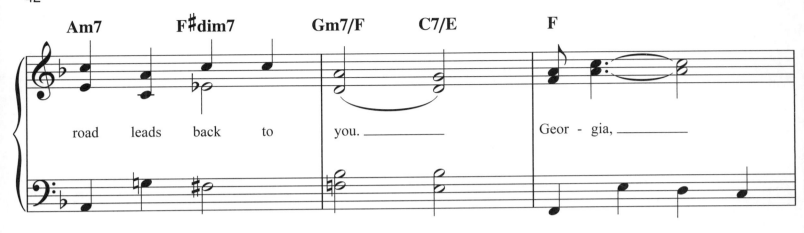

road leads back to you. _____ Geor - gia, _____

Geor - gia, _____ no peace I find. Just an

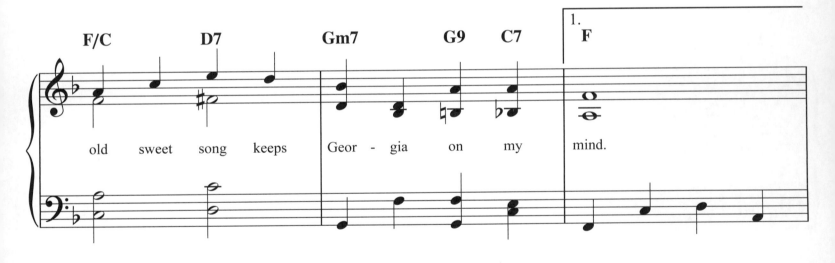

old sweet song keeps Geor - gia on my mind.

mind. _____

I CAN'T GET STARTED

from ZIEGFELD FOLLIES

Words by IRA GERSHWIN
Music by VERNON DUKE

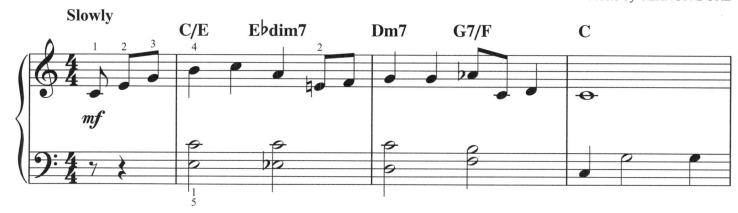

I've flown a - round the world in a plane; ____ I've set - tled

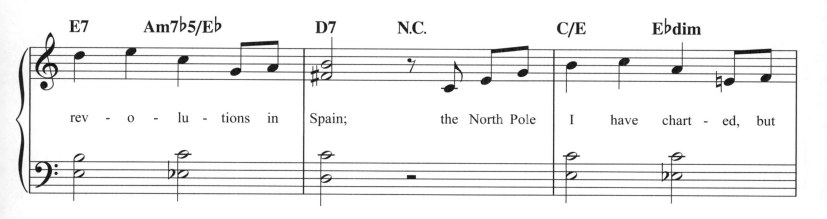

rev - o - lu - tions in Spain; the North Pole I have chart - ed, but

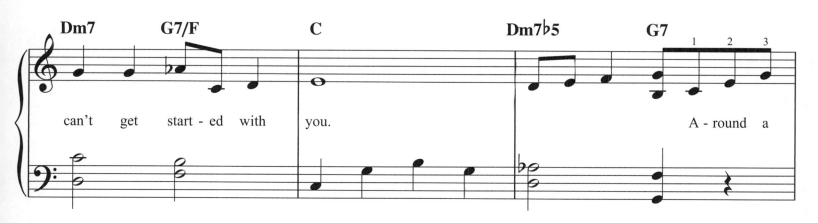

can't get start - ed with you.

A - round a

44

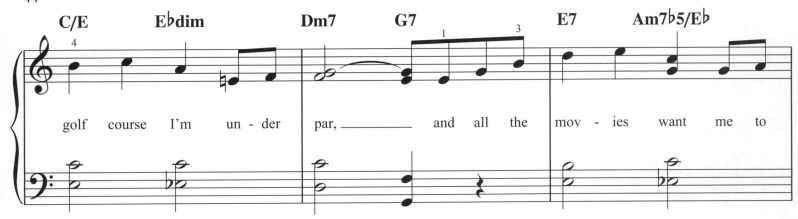

golf course I'm un - der par, _____ and all the mov - ies want me to

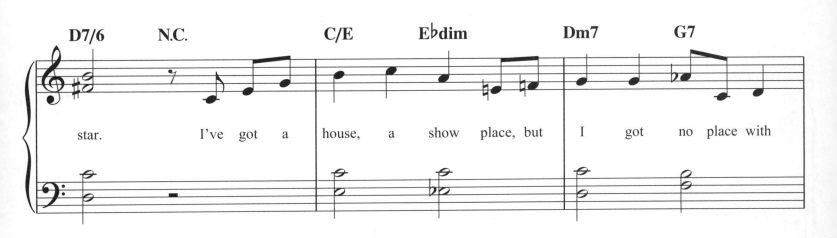

star. I've got a house, a show place, but I got no place with

you. You're so su - preme,

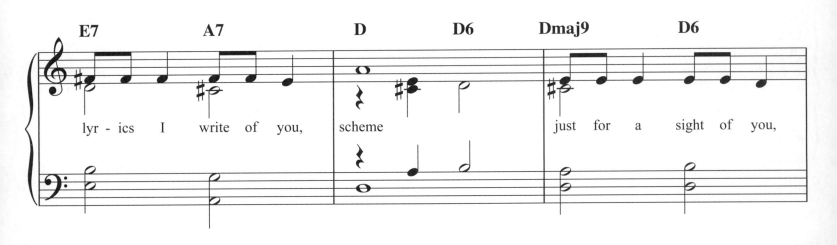

lyr - ics I write of you, scheme just for a sight of you,

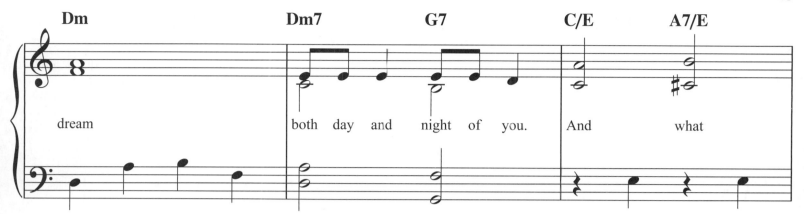

dream ___ both day and night of you. And what

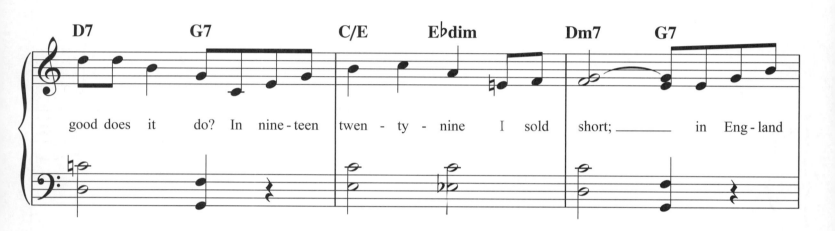

good does it do? In nine-teen twen-ty-nine I sold short; _____ in Eng-land

I'm pre-sent-ed at court, but you've got me down-heart-ed 'cause I

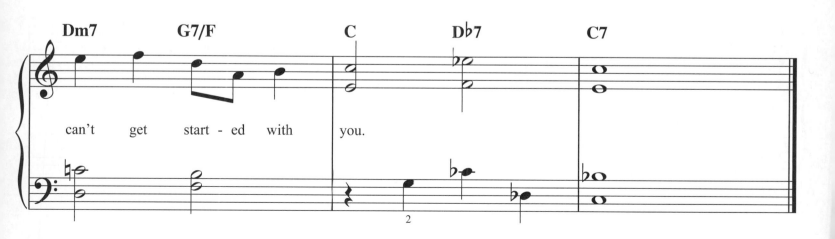

can't get start-ed with you.

THE GIRL FROM IPANEMA
(Garôta De Ipanema)

Music by ANTONIO CARLOS JOBIM
English Words by NORMAN GIMBEL
Original Words by VINICIUS DE MORAES

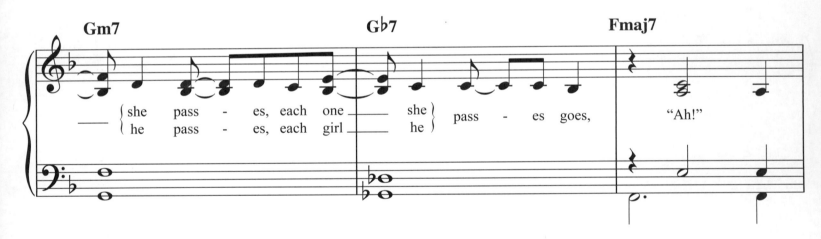

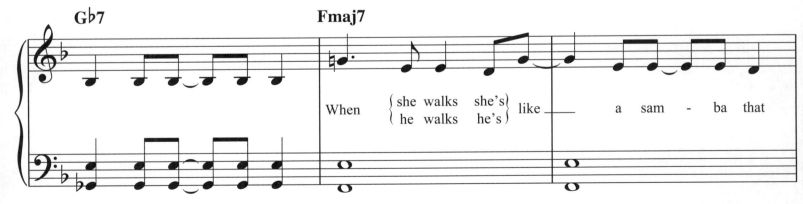

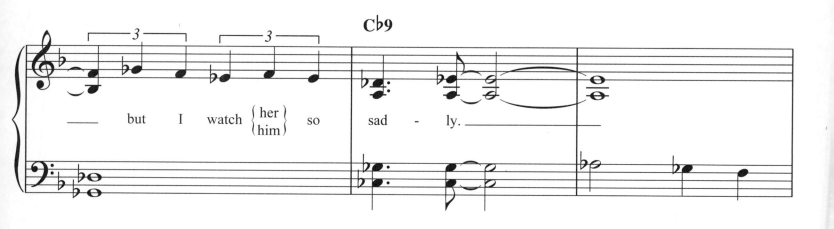

48

How _____ can I tell {her}{him} I love {her?}{him?} _____

_____ } Yes, _____ I would give my heart

glad - ly, _____ but each day when {she}{he} walks to the

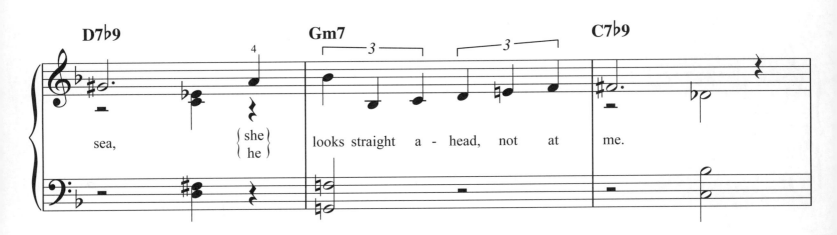

sea, {she}{he} looks straight a - head, not at me.

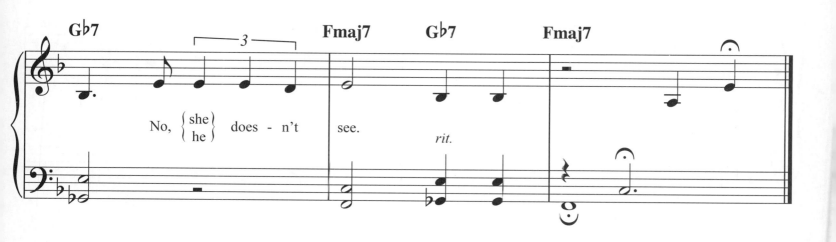

HOW HIGH THE MOON

from TWO FOR THE SHOW

Lyrics by NANCY HAMILTON
Music by MORGAN LEWIS

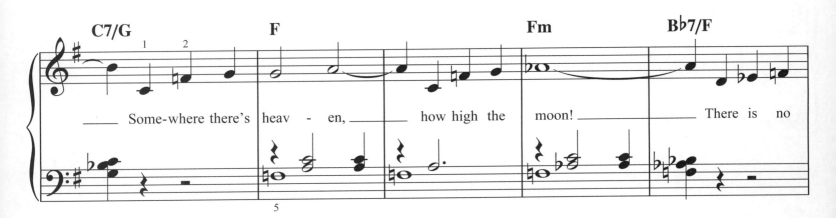

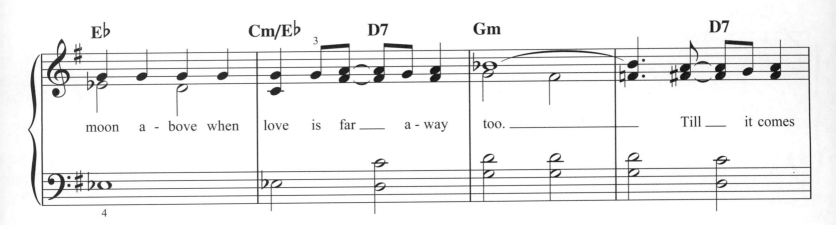

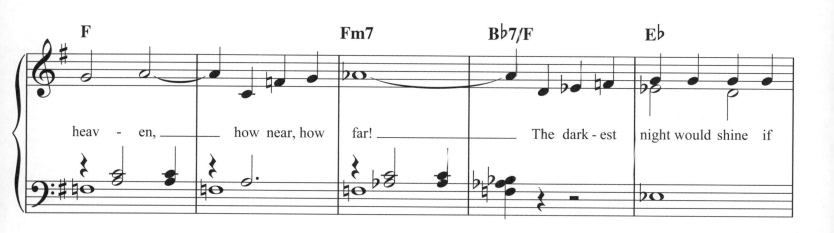

I GOT RHYTHM

from AN AMERICAN IN PARIS

Music and Lyrics by GEORGE GERSHWIN
and IRA GERSHWIN

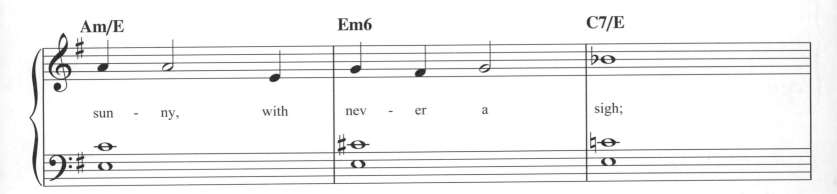

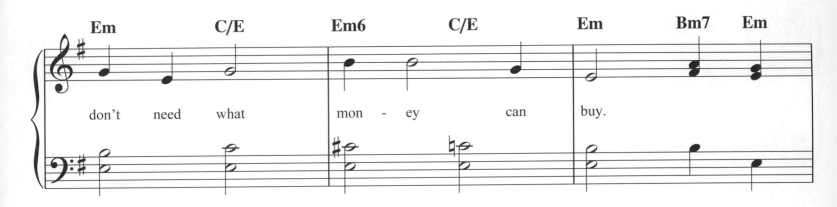

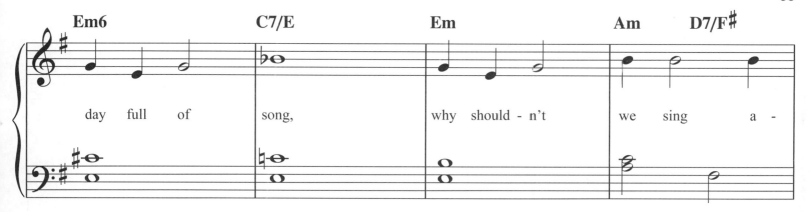

day full of song, why should-n't we sing a-

long? I'm chip - per

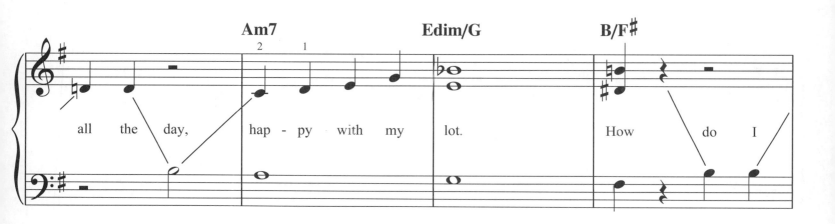

all the day, hap - py with my lot. How do I

get that way? Look at what I've got:

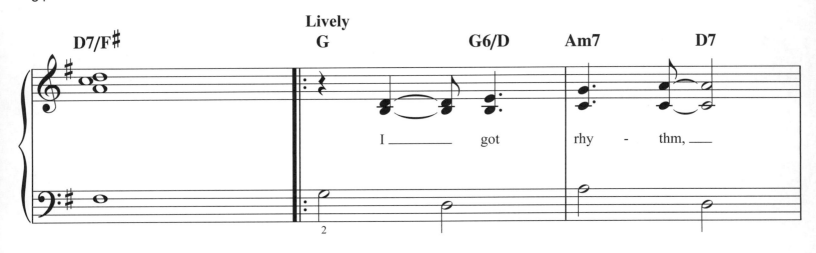

Lively

I _____ got rhy - thm, ___

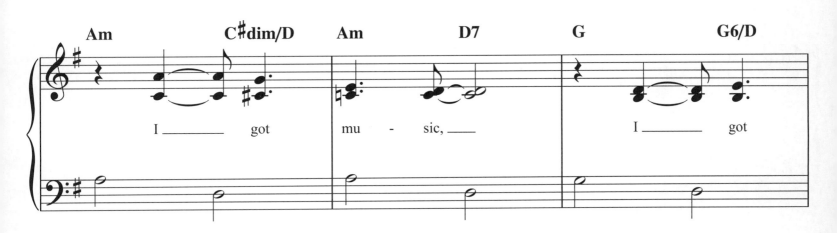

I _____ got mu - sic, ___ I _____ got

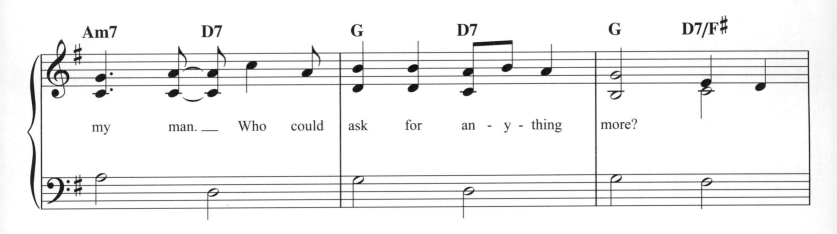

my man. ___ Who could ask for an - y - thing more?

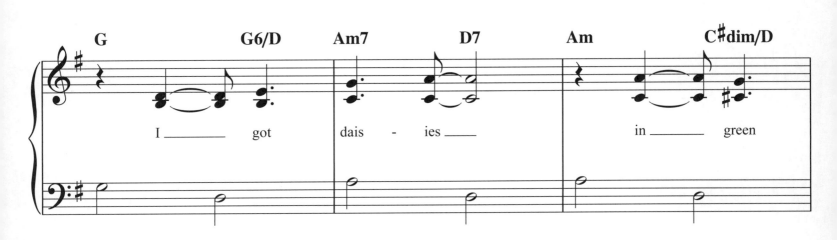

I _____ got dais - ies ___ in _____ green

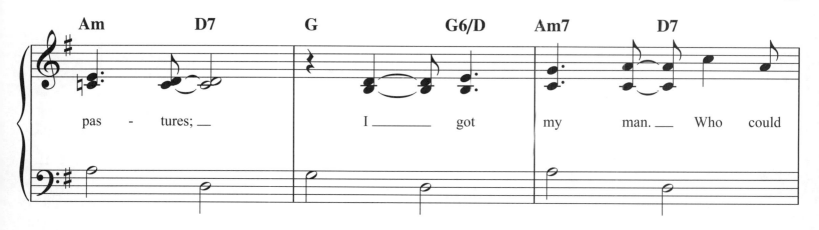

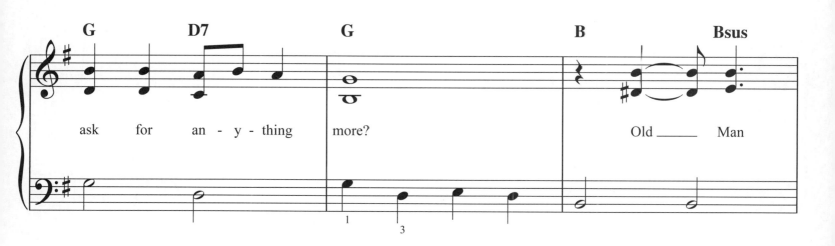

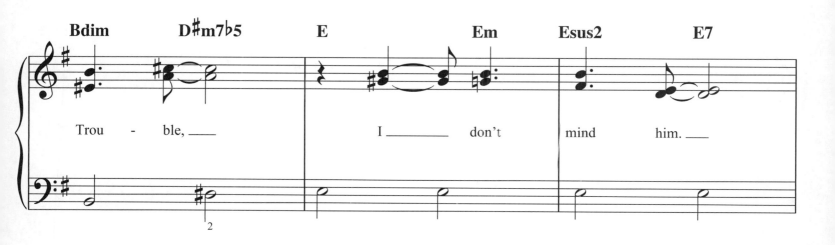

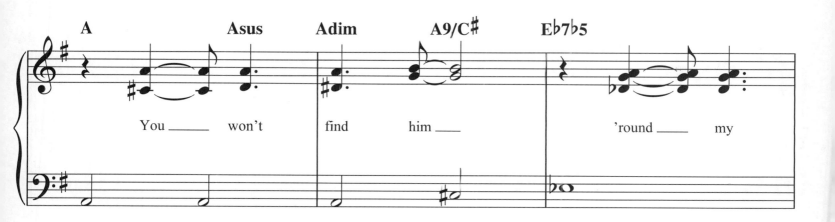

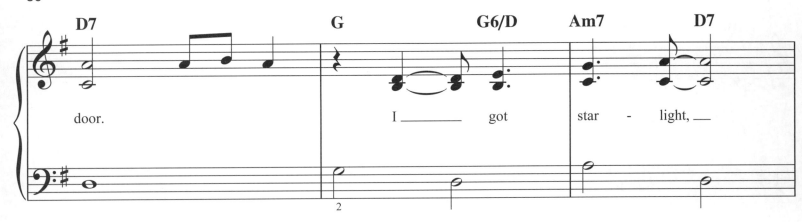

door.
I _____ got star - light, ___

I _____ got sweet dreams, ___ I _____ got

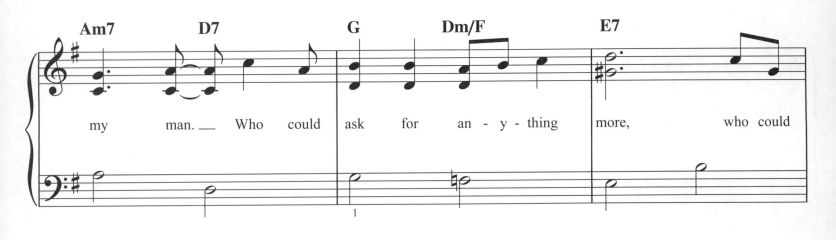

my man. ___ Who could ask for an - y - thing more, who could

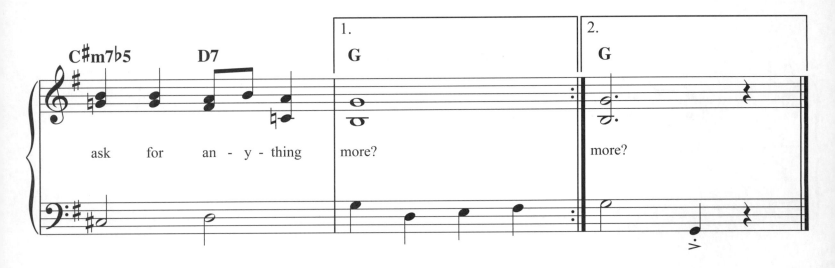

ask for an - y - thing more? more?

I'LL REMEMBER APRIL

Words and Music by PAT JOHNSTON,
DON RAYE and GENE DE PAUL

Moderately, with expression

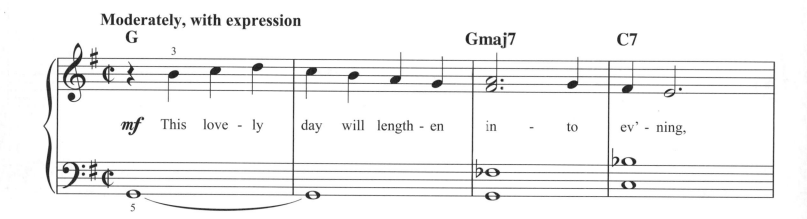

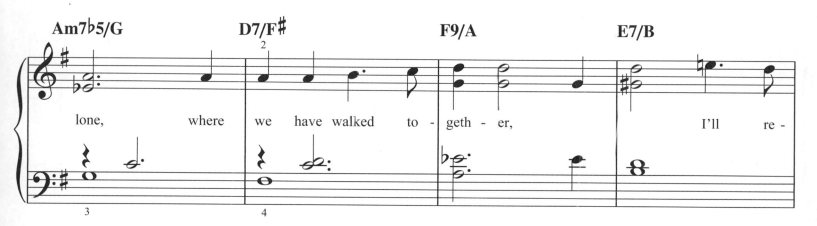

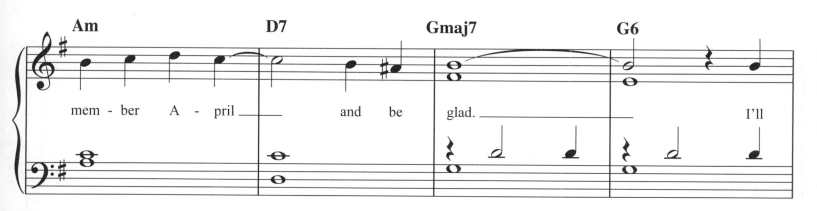

58

be con - tent _____ you loved me once in A - pril. Your

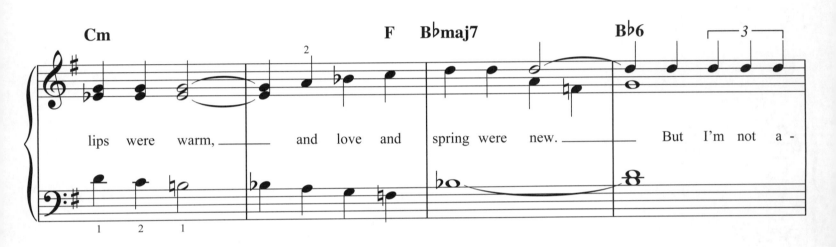

lips were warm, _____ and love and spring were new. _____ But I'm not a -

fraid of au - tumn and her sor - row, _____ for I'll re -

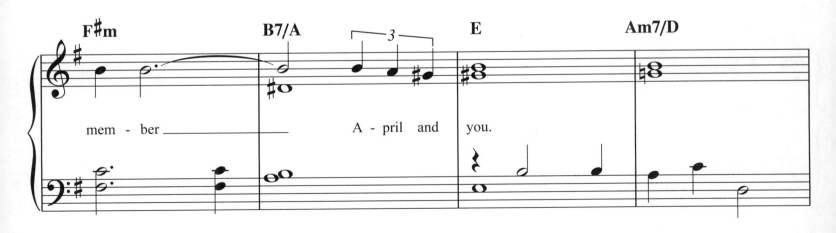

mem - ber _____ A - pril and you.

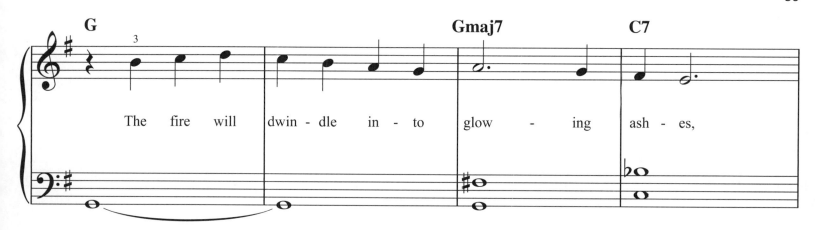

G   **Gmaj7**   **C7**

The fire will dwin - dle in - to glow - ing ash - es,

Gm7/F   **Gm6/E**   **Gm7/D**   **Gm6/E**

for flames and love live such a lit - tle while. _____ I

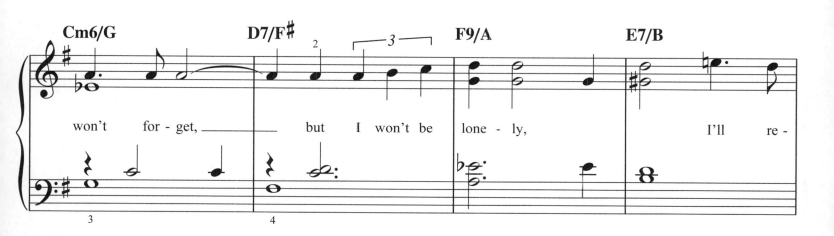

Cm6/G   **D7/F#**   **F9/A**   **E7/B**

won't for - get, _____ but I won't be lone - ly, I'll re -

Am   **D7**   **G N.C.**   **C13#11**

mem - ber A - pril, ___ and I'll smile. *rit.*

IF I SHOULD LOSE YOU
from the Paramount Picture ROSE OF THE RANCHO

Words and Music by LEO ROBIN
and RALPH RAINGER

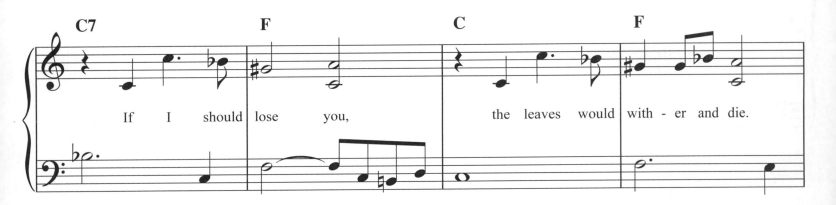

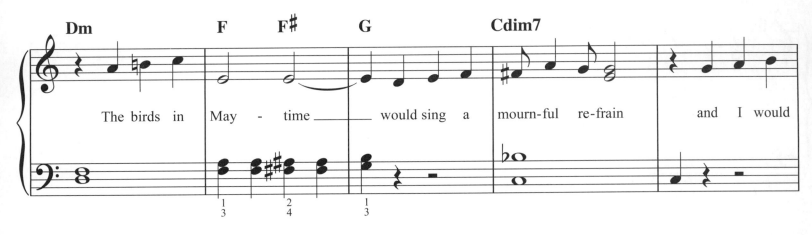

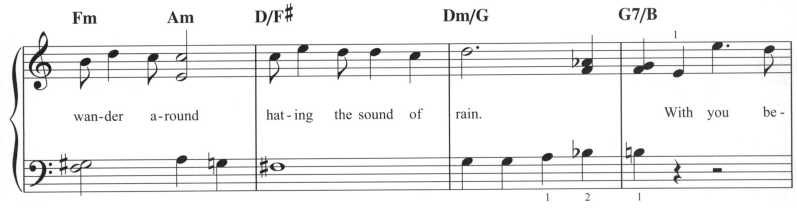

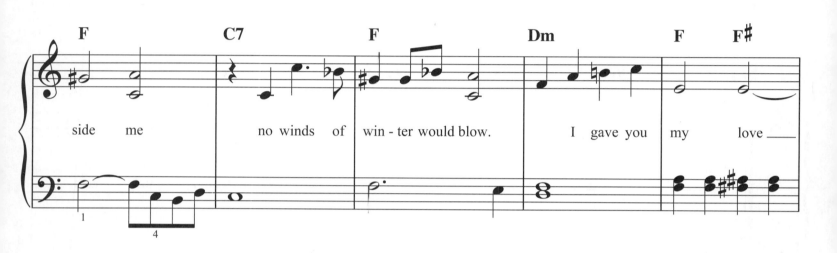

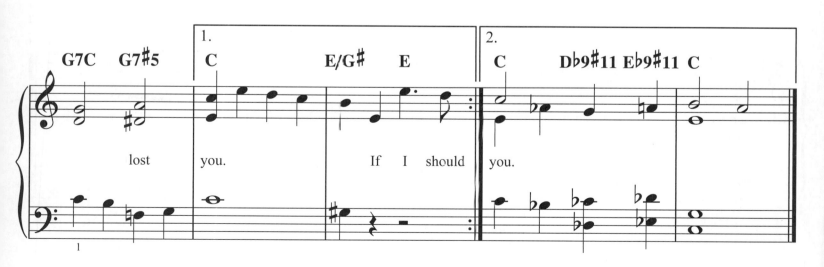

IN A SENTIMENTAL MOOD

Words and Music by DUKE ELLINGTON,
IRVING MILLS and MANNY KURTZ

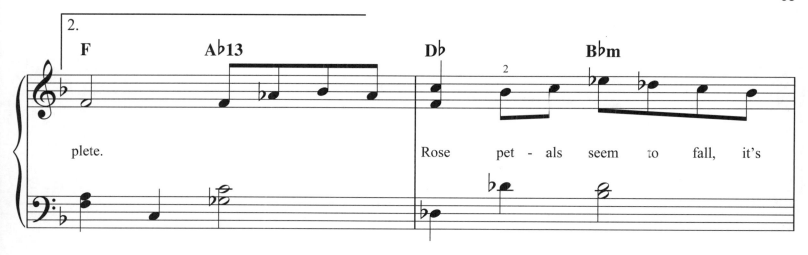

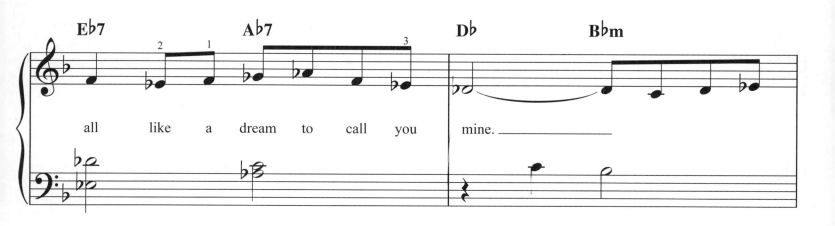

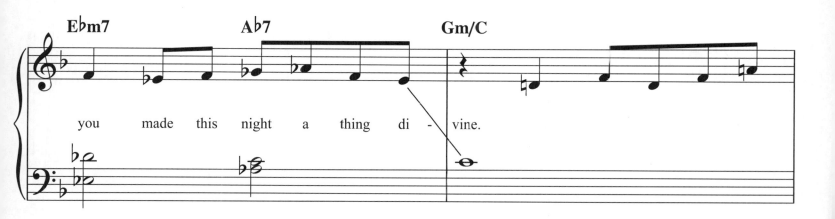

64

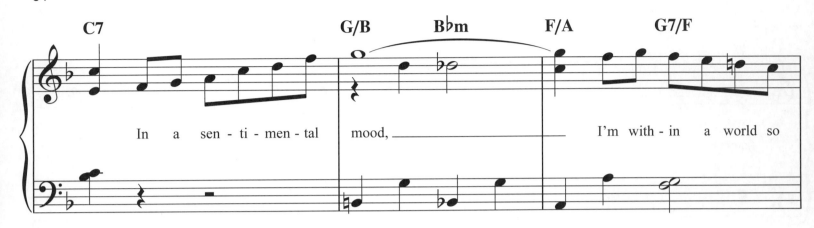

In a sen - ti - men - tal mood, _____ I'm with - in a world so

heav - en - ly, _____ for I nev - er dreamt that you'd _____ be lov - ing

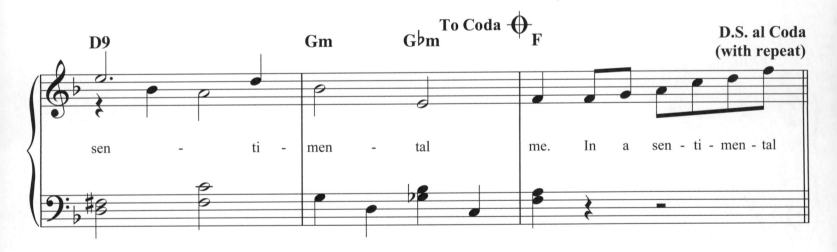

sen - ti - men - tal me. In a sen - ti - men - tal

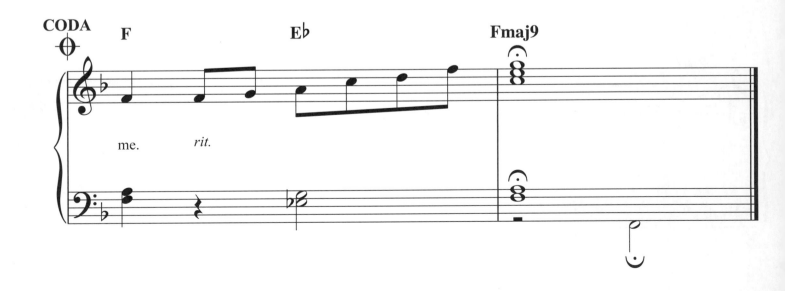

me. *rit.*

IT COULD HAPPEN TO YOU

from the Paramount Picture AND THE ANGELS SING

Words by JOHNNY BURKE
Music by JAMES VAN HEUSEN

Lyrics: Hide your heart from sight, lock your dreams at night, it could hap-pen to you.

Am   **Cm/E♭**   **G/D**

Don't count stars or you might stum - ble, _____

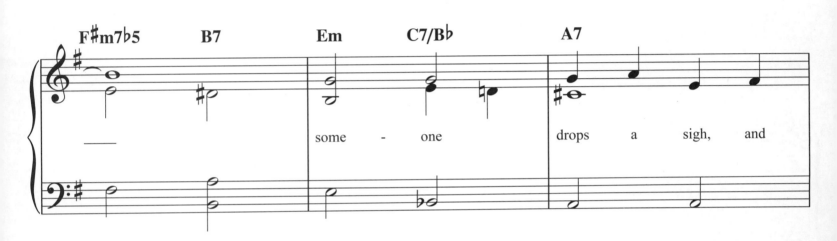

F♯m7♭5   **B7**   **Em**   **C7/B♭**   **A7**

_____ some - one drops a sigh, and

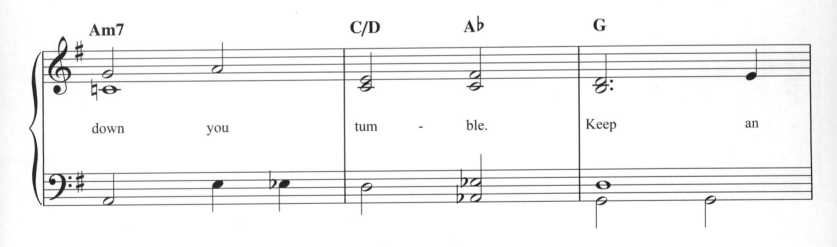

Am7   **C/D**   **A♭**   **G**

down you tum - ble. Keep an

G♯dim   **Am**   **A♯dim**

eye on spring, run when church bells ring,

JUST FRIENDS

Lyrics by SAM M. LEWIS
Music by JOHN KLENNER

69

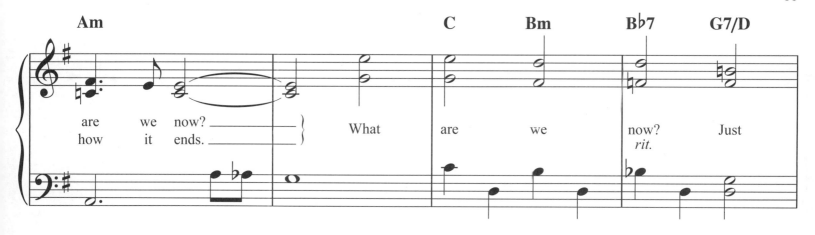

are we now? _____
how it ends. _____

What are we now? Just

With a lilt (♪♪ = ♪♪)

friends, _____ lov - ers no more; _____ just

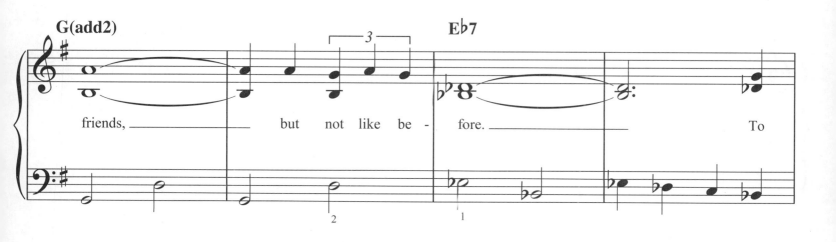

friends, _____ but not like be - fore. _____ To

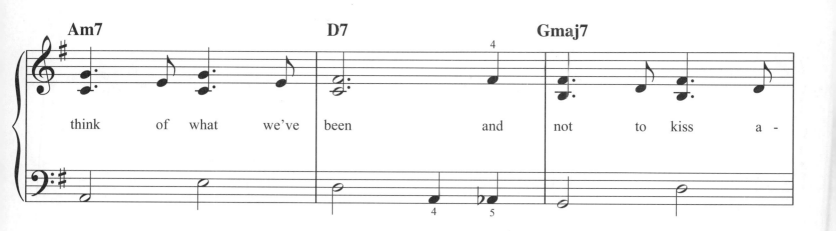

think of what we've been and not to kiss a -

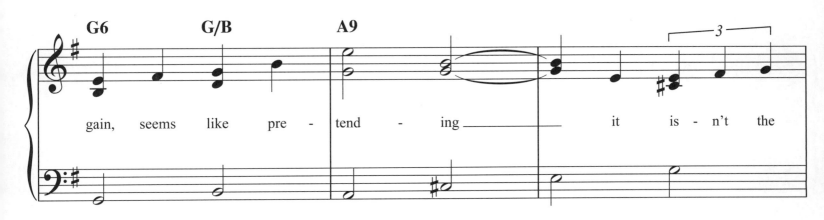

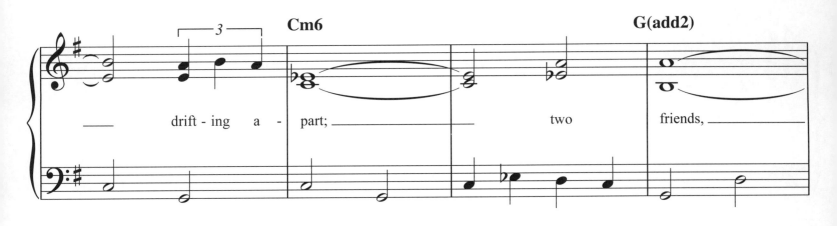

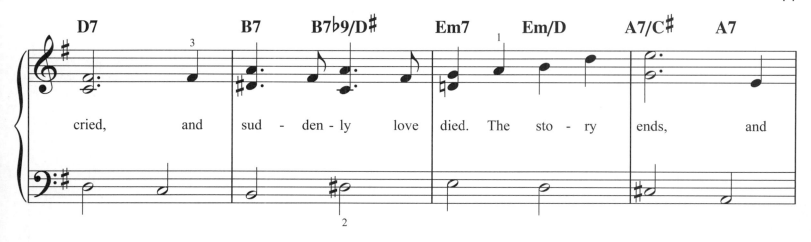

cried,   and   sud - den - ly   love   died.   The   sto - ry   ends,   and

we're   just   friends.   *rit.*

friends.   Just

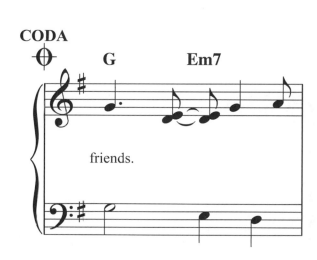

friends.

LAURA

Lyrics by JOHNNY MERCER
Music by DAVID RAKSIN

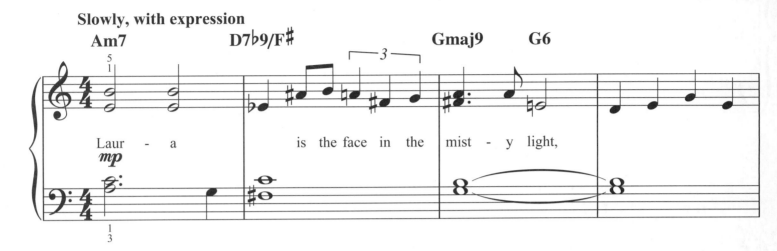

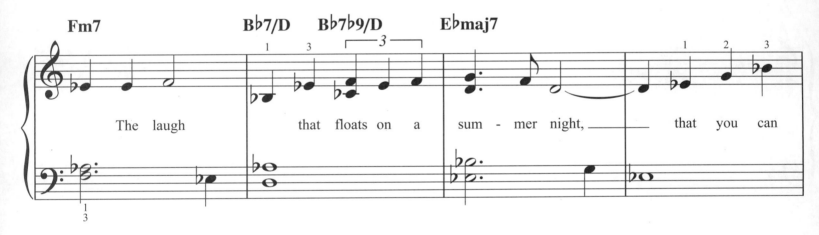

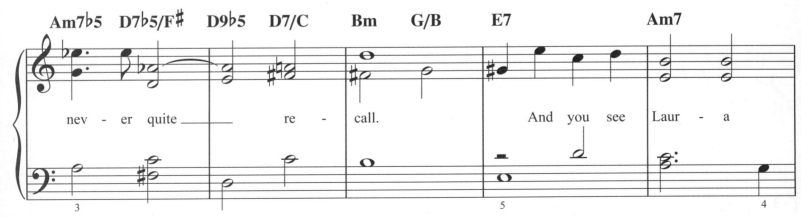

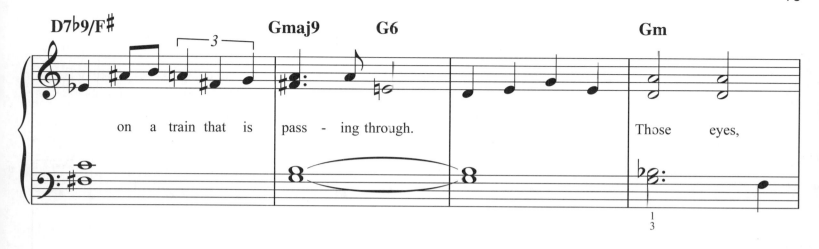

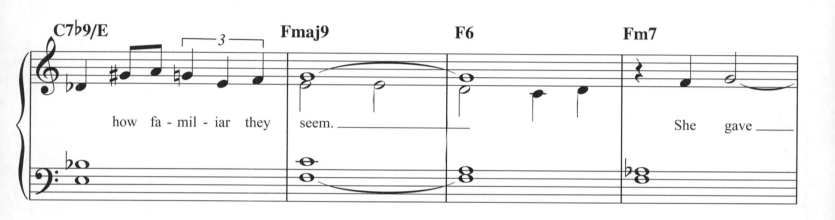

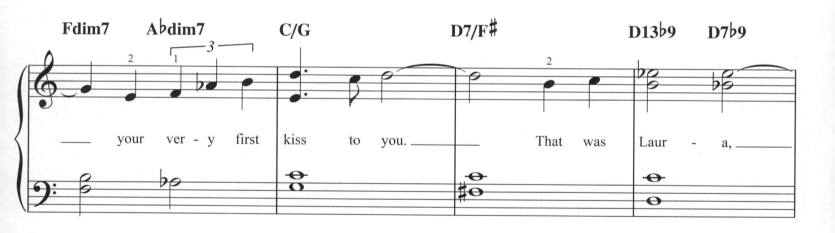

LOVER MAN
(Oh, Where Can You Be?)

Words and Music by JIMMY DAVIS,
ROGER RAMIREZ and JIMMY SHERMAN

I'd give my soul just to call you my own. __ Got a moon a-bove me,

but no one to love me, Lov-er Man, oh where can you be?

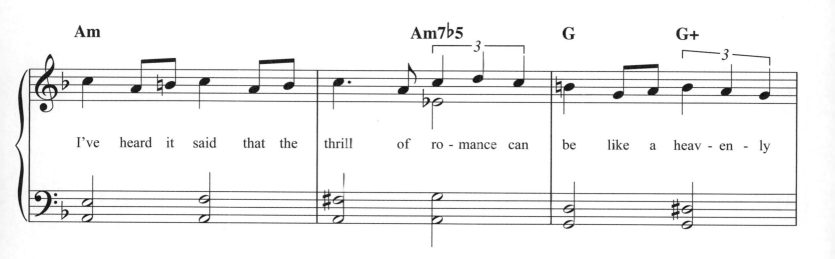

I've heard it said that the thrill of ro-mance can be like a heav-en-ly

dream. I go to bed with a pray'r that you'll make love to

MY ONE AND ONLY LOVE

Words by ROBERT MELLIN
Music by GUY WOOD

78

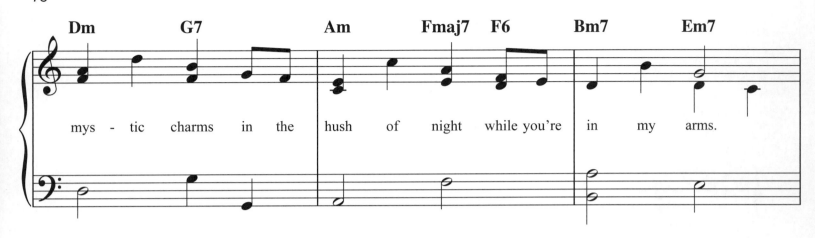

ev - er I speak tells me that you are my own.

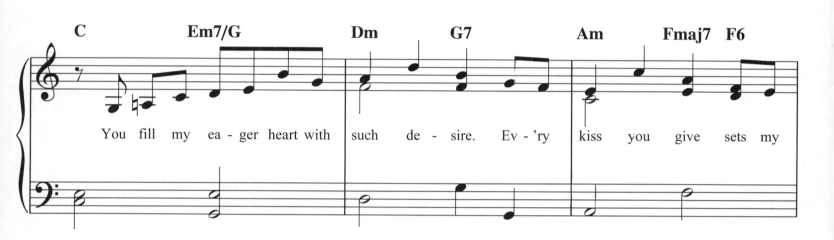

You fill my ea - ger heart with such de - sire. Ev - 'ry kiss you give sets my

soul on fire. I give my - self in sweet sur - ren - der,

my one and on - ly love. love.

MISTY

Words by JOHNNY BURKE
Music by ERROLL GARNER

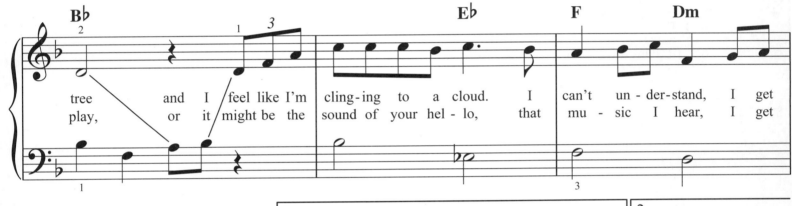

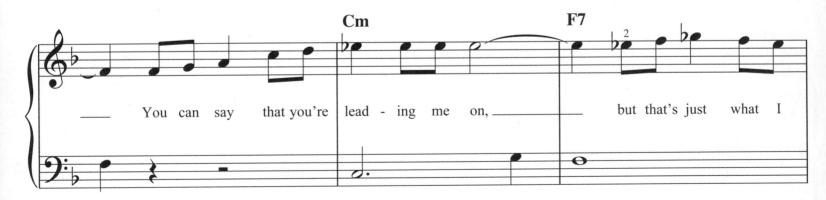

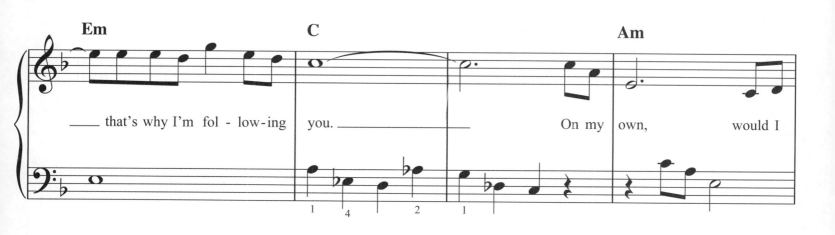

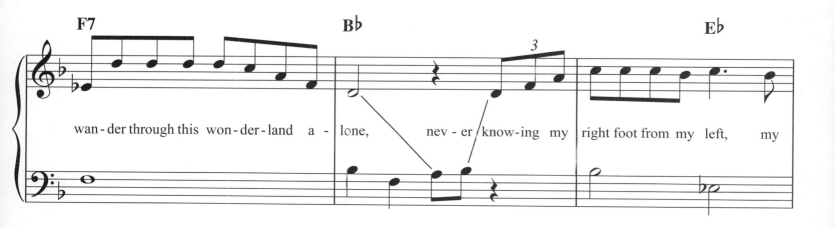

MOONLIGHT IN VERMONT

Words by JOHN BLACKBURN
Music by KARL SUESSDORF

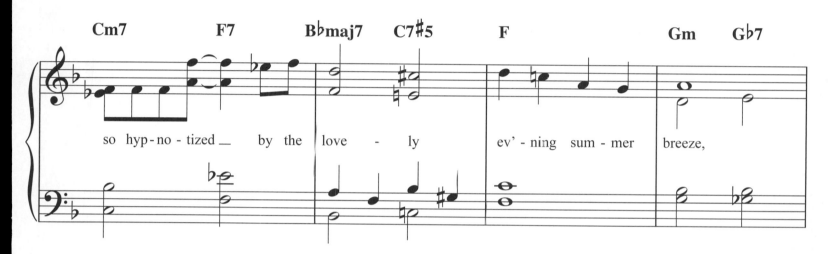

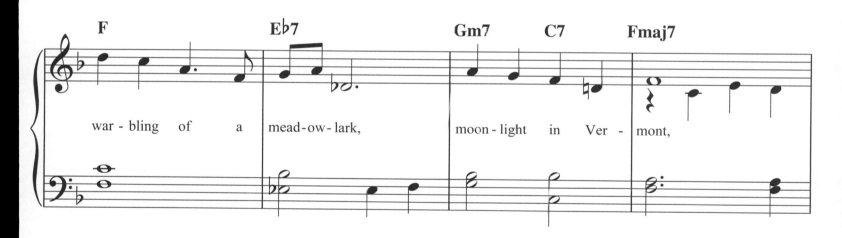

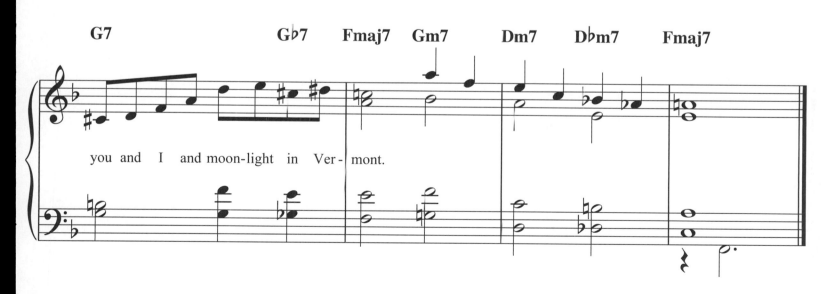

MY FUNNY VALENTINE

from BABES IN ARMS

Words by LORENZ HART
Music by RICHARD RODGERS

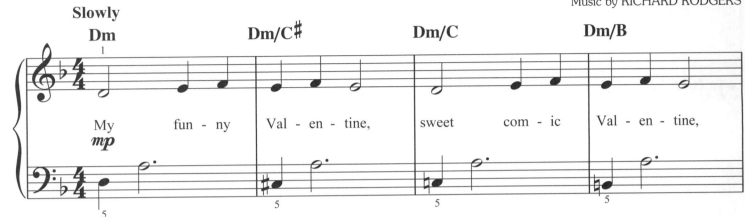

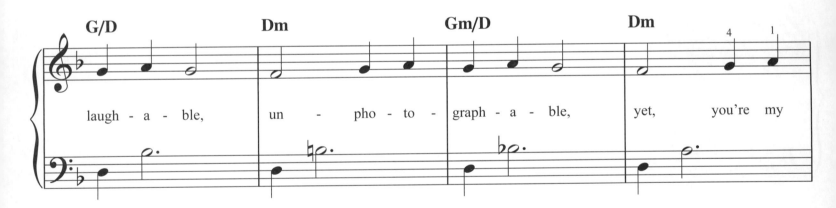

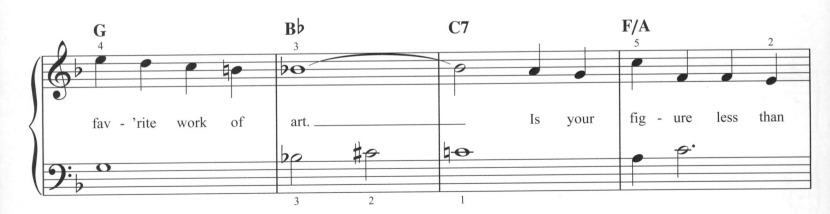

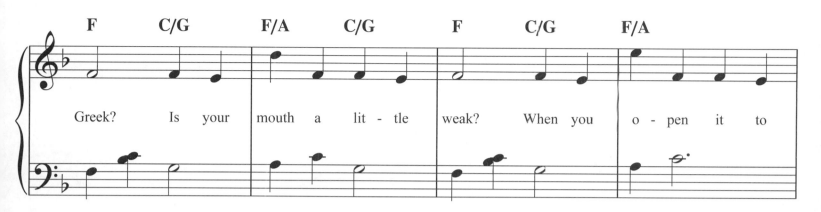

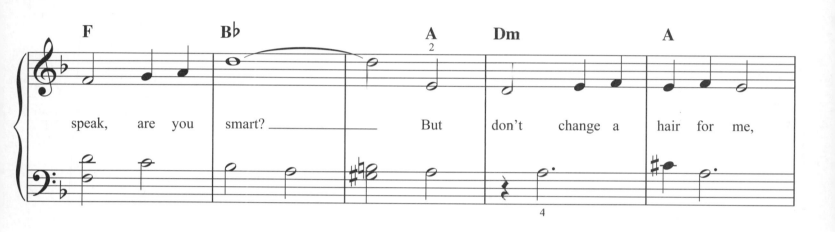

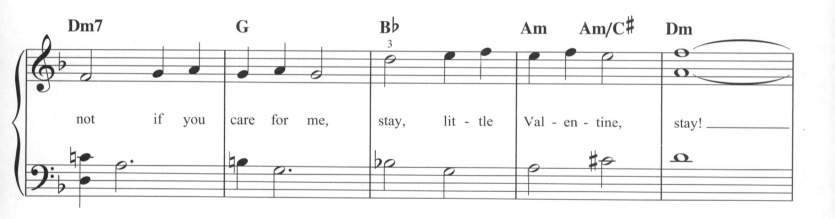

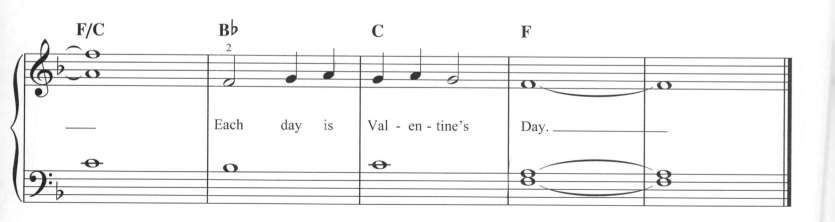

MY ROMANCE
from JUMBO

Words by LORENZ HART
Music by RICHARD RODGERS

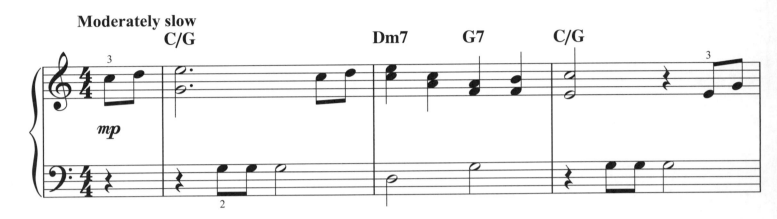

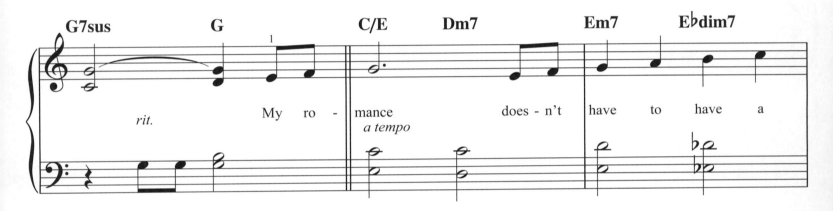

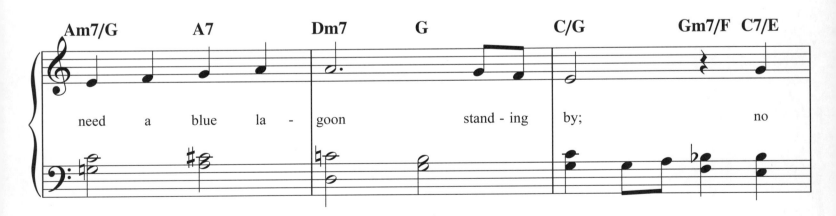

87

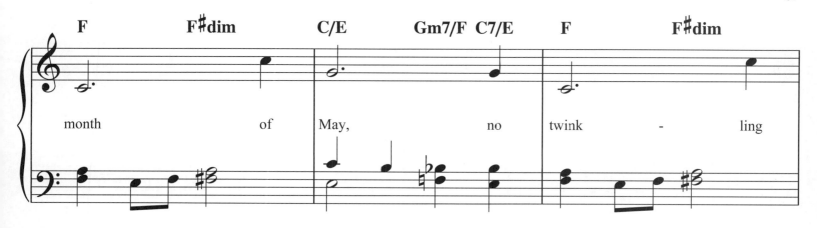

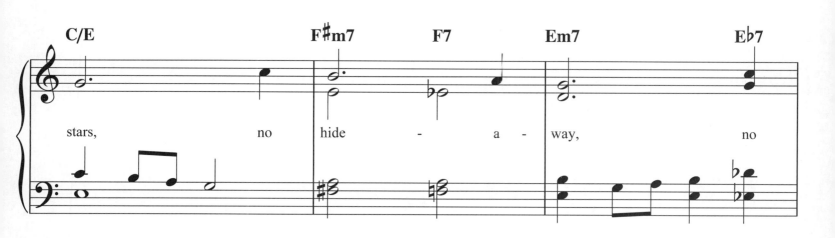

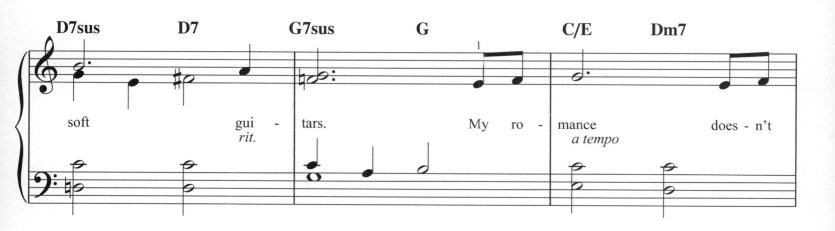

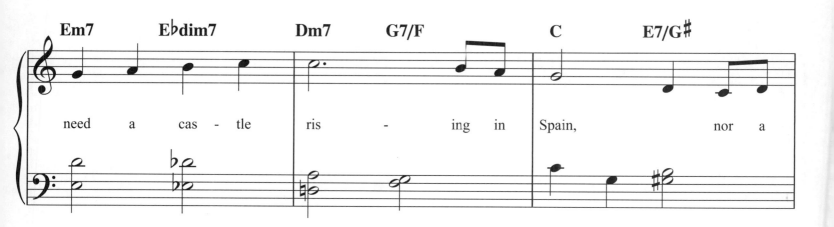

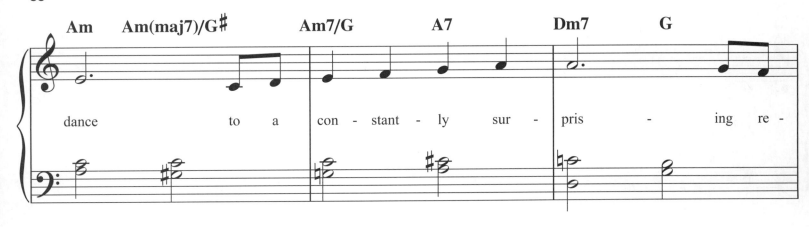

dance to a con - stant - ly sur - pris - ing re -

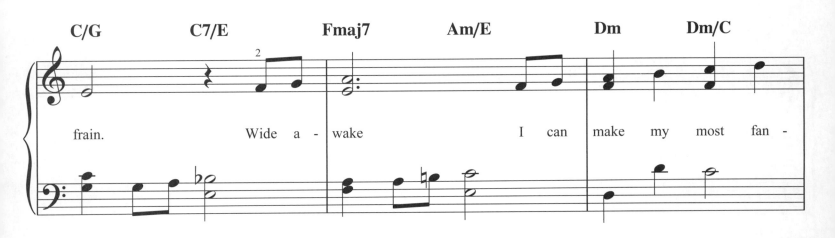

frain. Wide a - wake I can make my most fan -

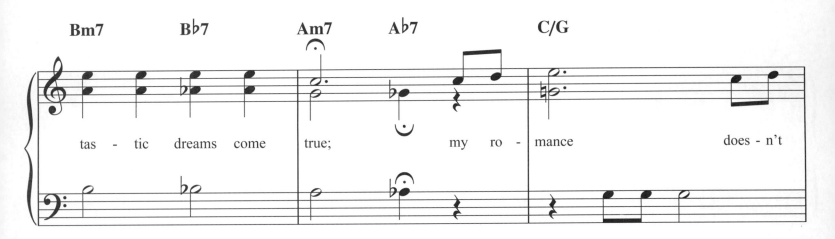

tas - tic dreams come true; my ro - mance does - n't

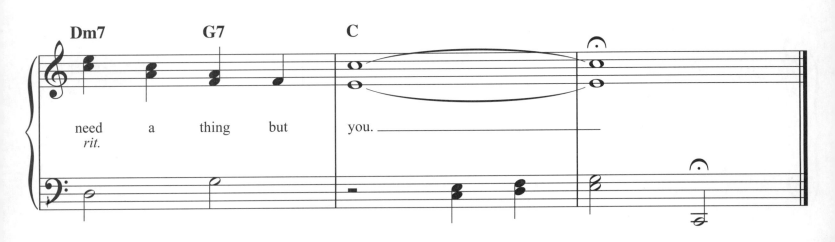

need a thing but you.

rit.

THE NEARNESS OF YOU
from the Paramount Picture ROMANCE IN THE DARK

Words by NED WASHINGTON
Music by HOAGY CARMICHAEL

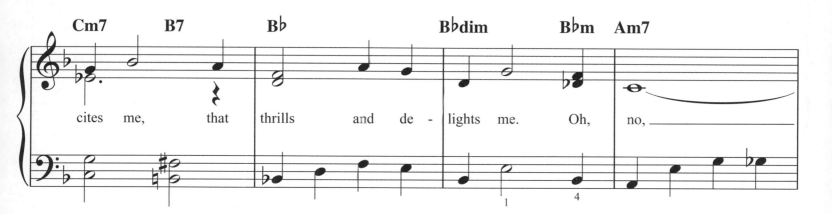

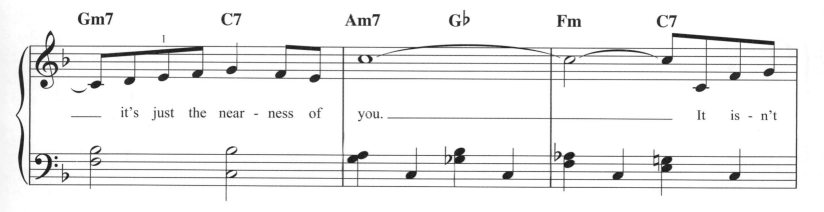

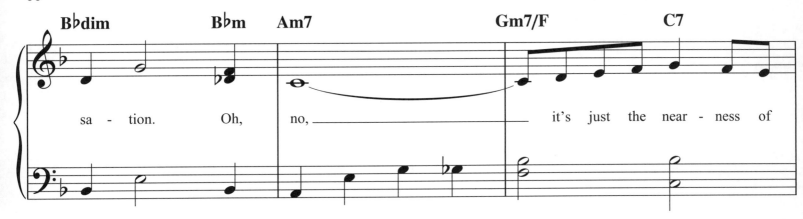

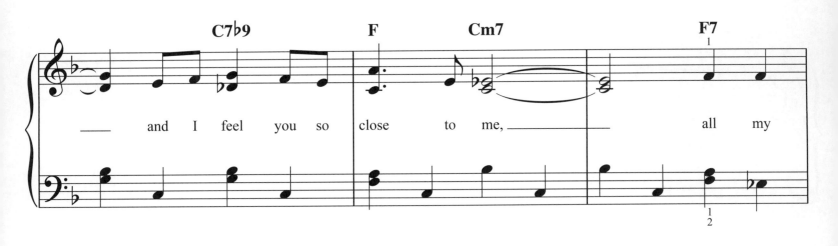

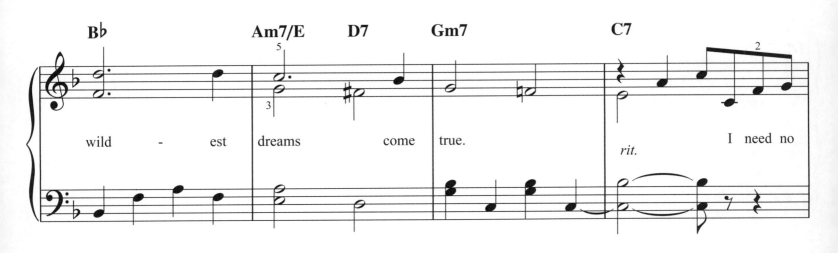

Fmaj7   **Cm7**   **B7**   **B♭**   **B♭dim**   **B♭m**

soft   lights   to en -   chant me   if   you'll   on - ly   grant me   the

a tempo

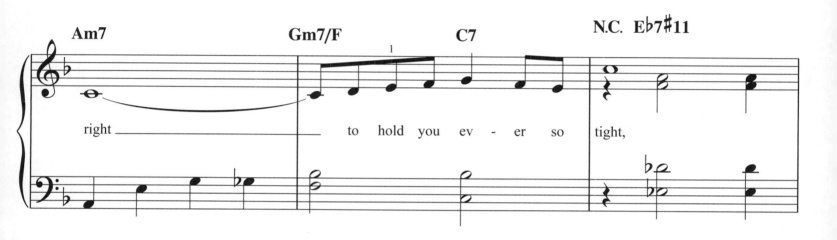

Am7   **Gm7/F**   **C7**   **N.C. E♭7#11**

right _____   to hold you ev - er so   tight,

D7   **B♭**   **C7**

and   to feel   in   the   night   the   near - ness   of

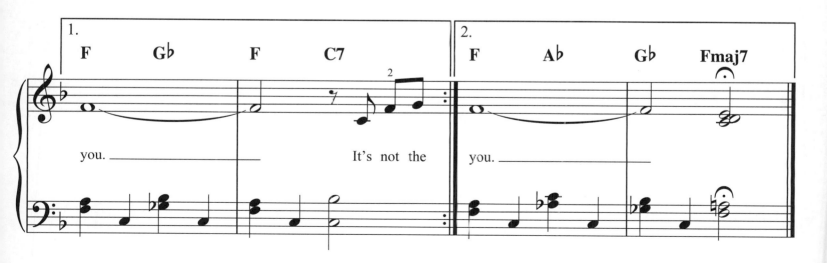

1.

F   **G♭**   **F**   **C7**

you. _____   It's not the

2.

F   **A♭**   **G♭**   **Fmaj7**

you. _____

NIGHT AND DAY

Words and Music by
COLE PORTER

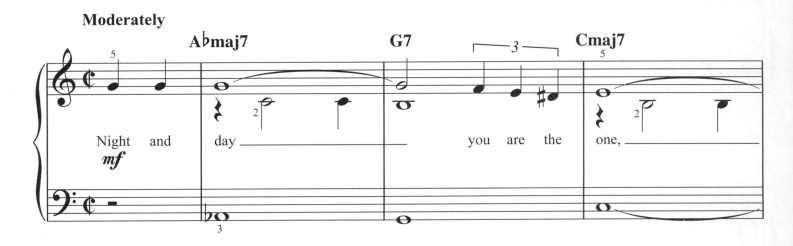

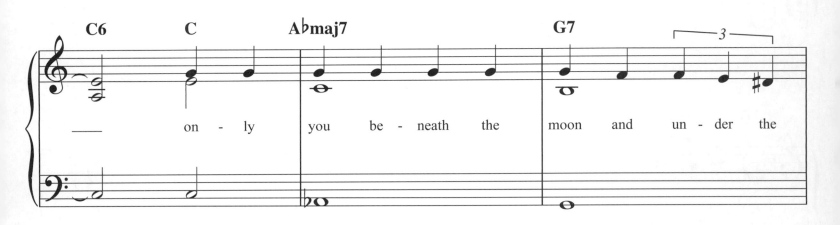

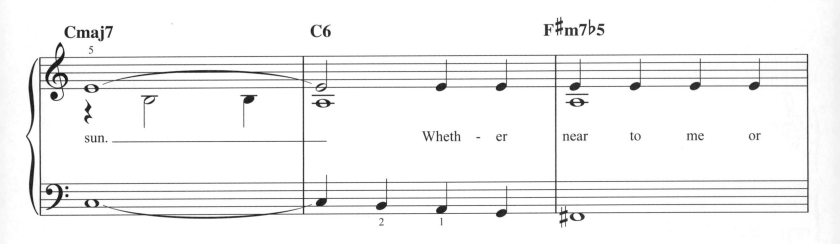

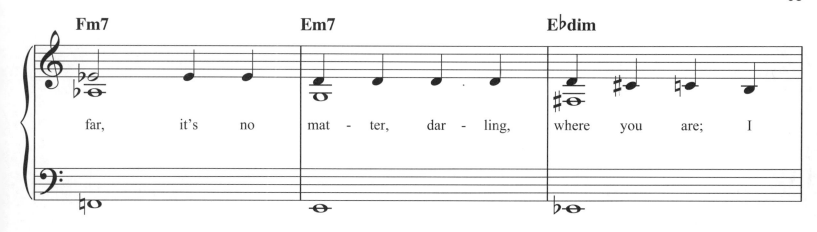

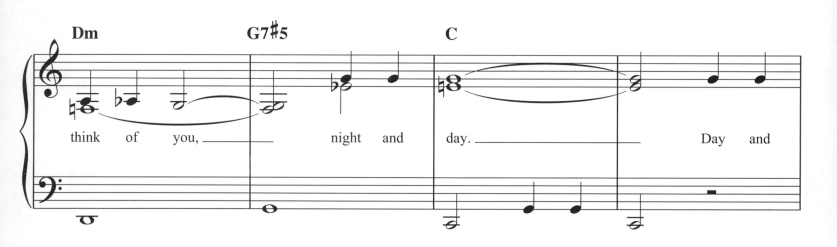

94

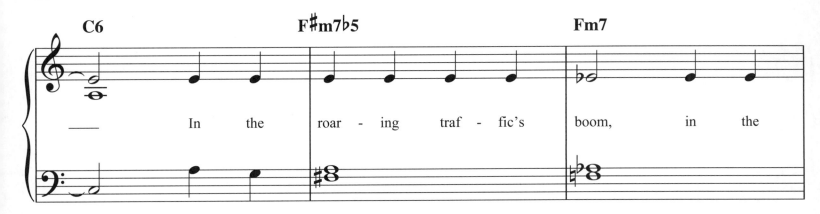

In the roar - ing traf - fic's boom, in the

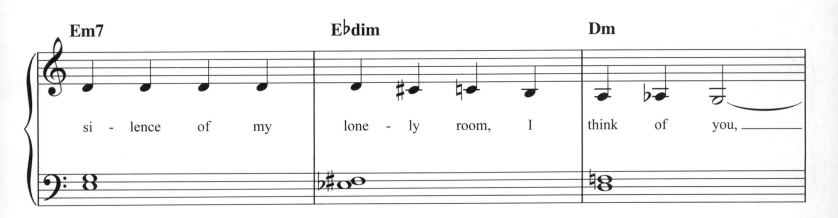

si - lence of my lone - ly room, I think of you, _____

_____ night and day. _____ Night and day, _____

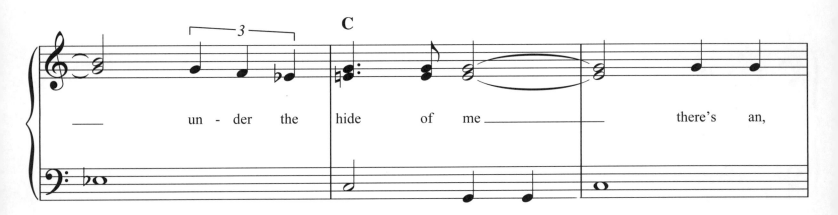

_____ un - der the hide of me _____ there's an,

oh, such a hun - gry yearn - ing burn - ing in - side of me. _____

_____ And its tor - ment won't be through 'til you

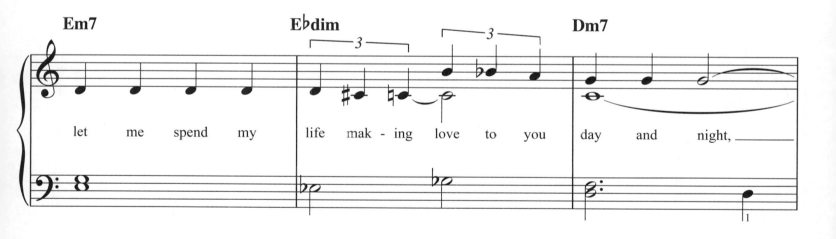

let me spend my life mak - ing love to you day and night, _____

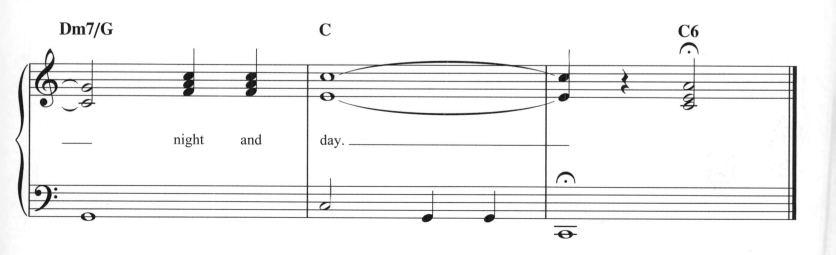

_____ night and day. _____

OUT OF NOWHERE

from the Paramount Picture DUDE RANCH

Words by EDWARD HEYMAN
Music by JOHNNY GREEN

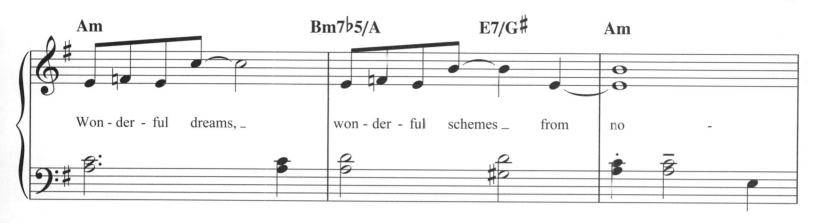

Am — Wonderful dreams, _ Bm7♭5/A — wonderful schemes _ from E7/G♯ Am no -

where — E♭7 made ev-'ry hour sweet as a flow-er for

Am7 me. _ D7 G If you should go _ back to your

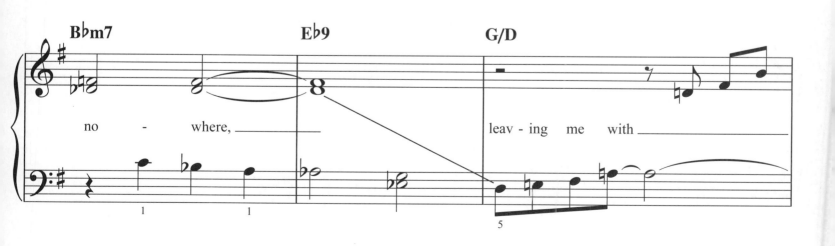

B♭m7 no - where, _ E♭9 G/D leav-ing me with _

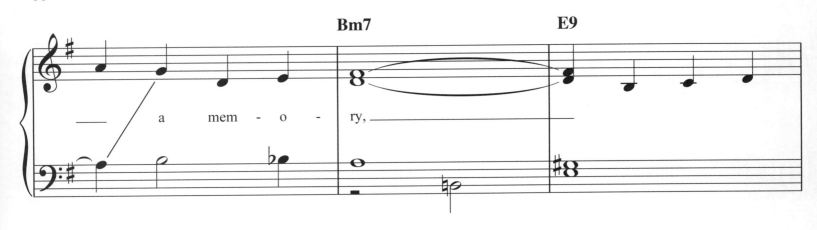

a mem - o - ry,

I'll al - ways wait for your re - turn out of no -

where, hop - ing you'll bring your love to

me. me. *rit.*

SATIN DOLL
from SOPHISTICATED LADIES

Words by JOHNNY MERCER
and BILLY STRAYHORN
Music by DUKE ELLINGTON

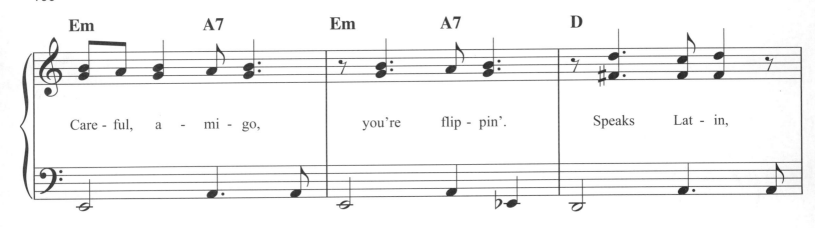

Careful, a - mi - go, you're flip - pin'. Speaks Lat - in,

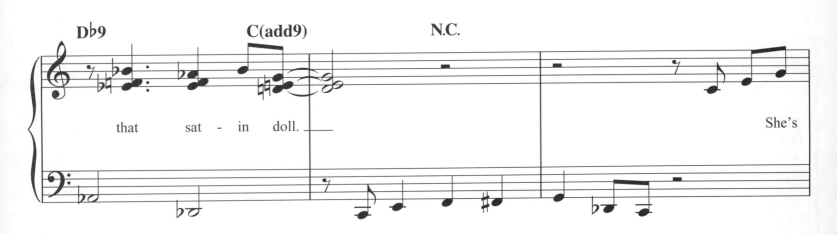

that sat - in doll. ___ She's

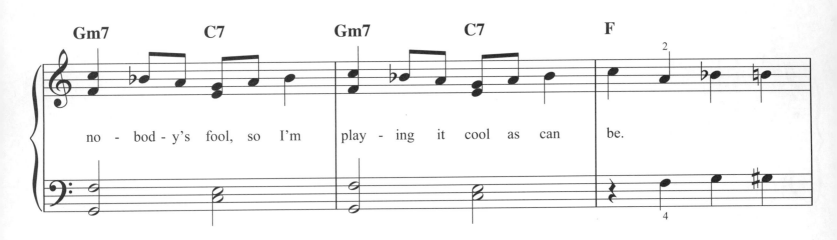

no - bod - y's fool, so I'm play - ing it cool as can be.

I'll give it a whirl, ___ but I ain't for no girl ___ catch - ing

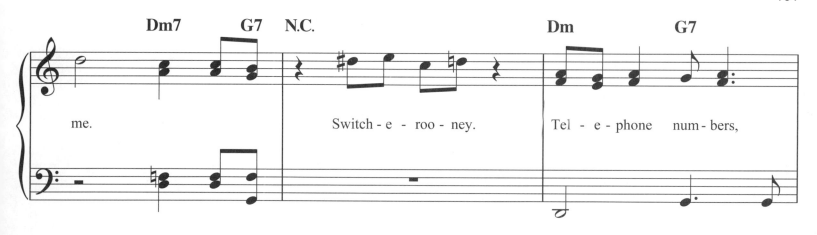

me.   Switch - e - roo - ney.   Tel - e - phone num - bers,

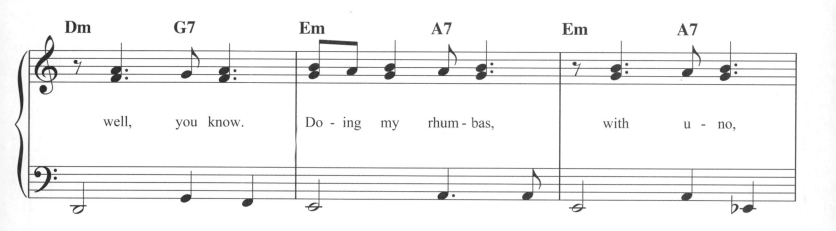

well,   you know.   Do - ing my rhum - bas,   with   u - no,

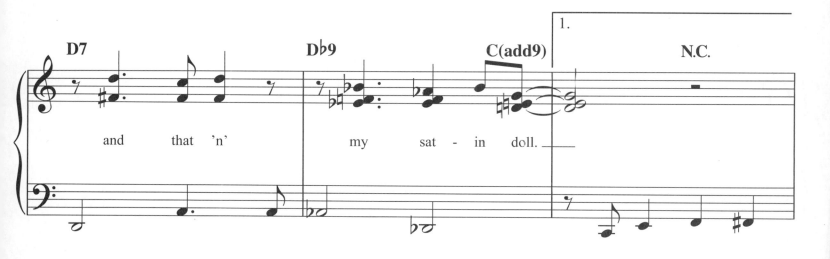

and   that 'n'   my sat - in doll.____

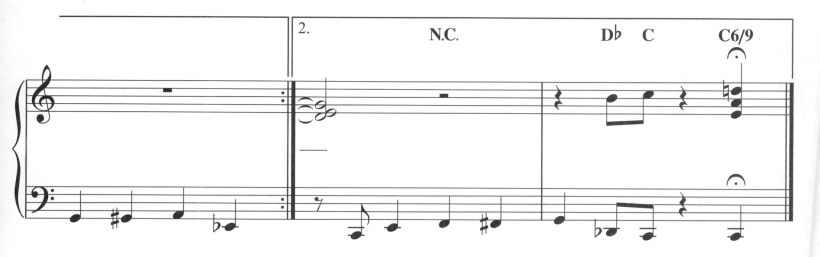

'ROUND MIDNIGHT

Words by BERNIE HANIGHEN
Music by THELONIOUS MONK
and COOTIE WILLIAMS

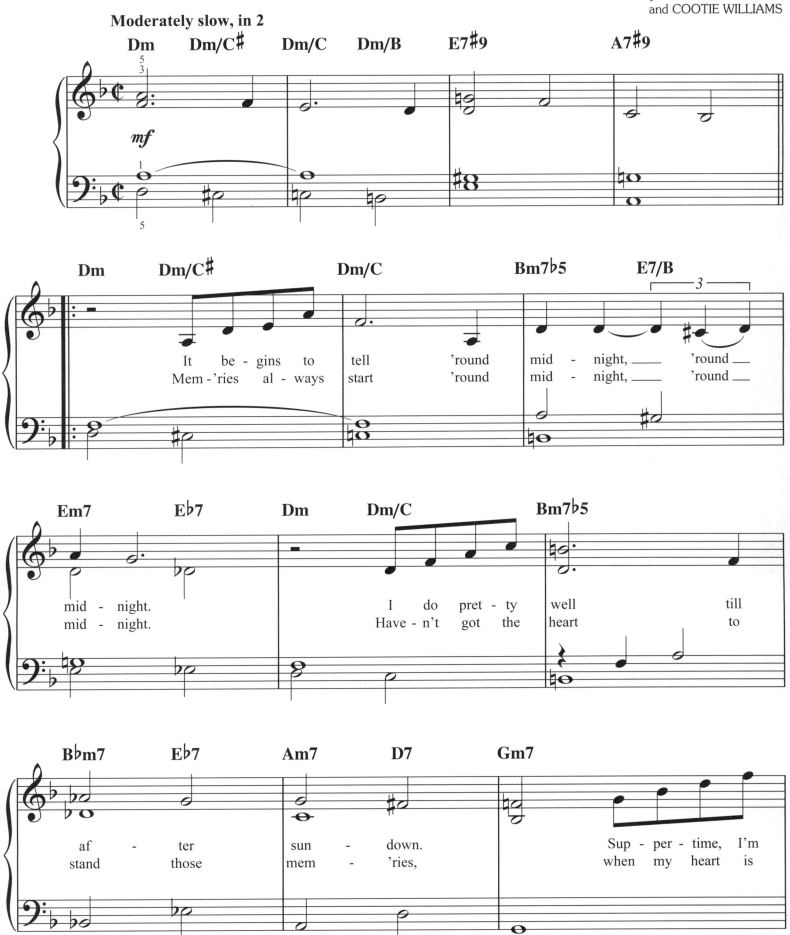

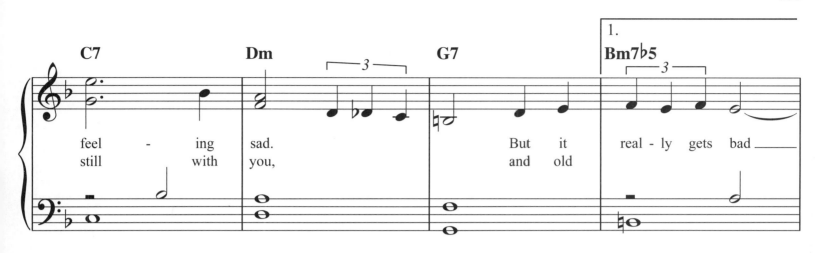

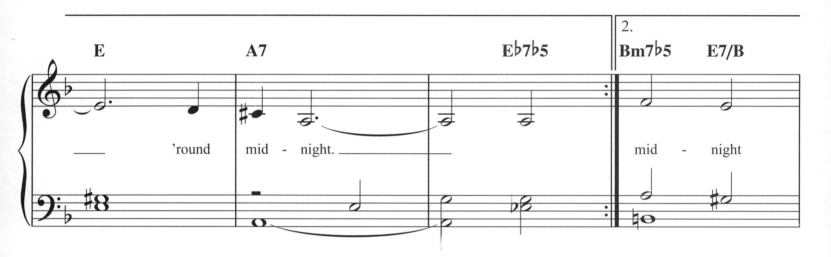

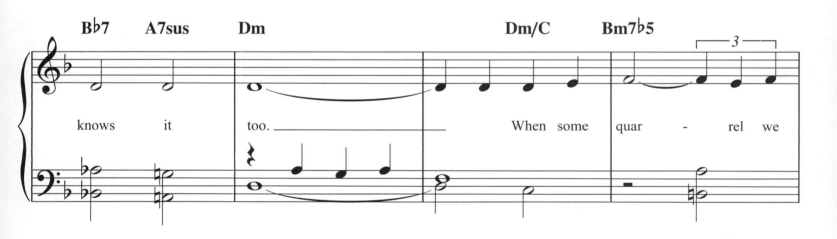

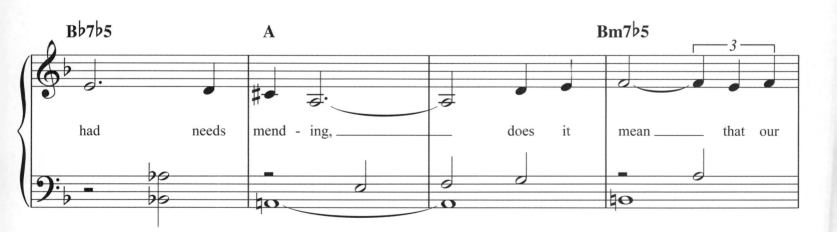

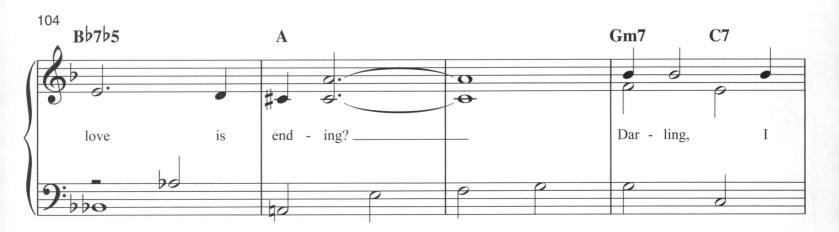

Bb7b5 ... **A** ... **Gm7** **C7**

love is end - ing? _____ Dar - ling, I

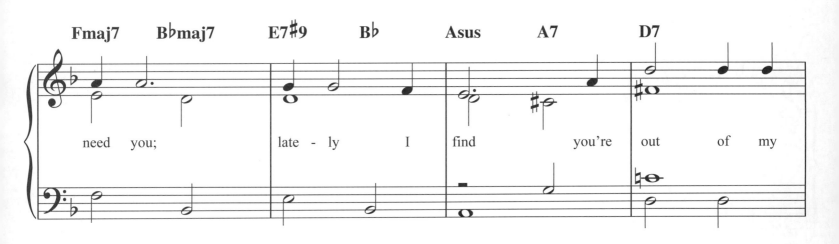

Fmaj7 **Bbmaj7** ... **E7#9** **Bb** ... **Asus** **A7** ... **D7**

need you; late - ly I find you're out of my

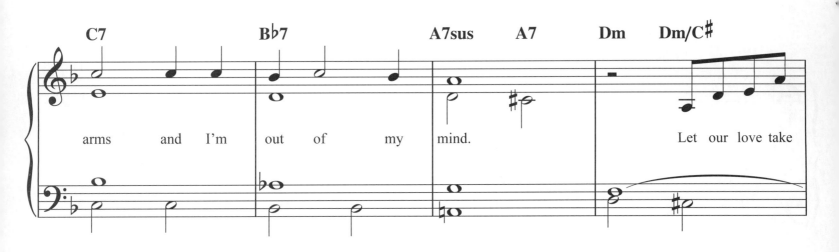

C7 ... **Bb7** ... **A7sus** **A7** ... **Dm** **Dm/C#**

arms and I'm out of my mind. Let our love take

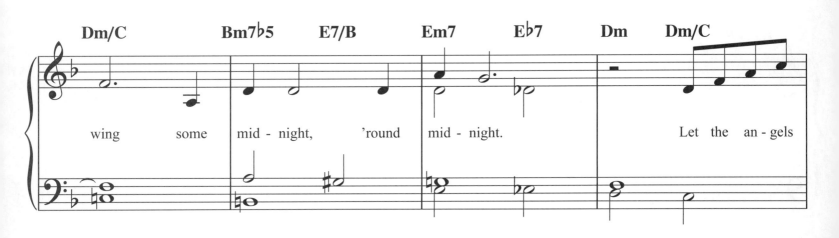

Dm/C ... **Bm7b5** **E7/B** ... **Em7** **Eb7** ... **Dm** **Dm/C**

wing some mid - night, 'round mid - night. Let the an - gels

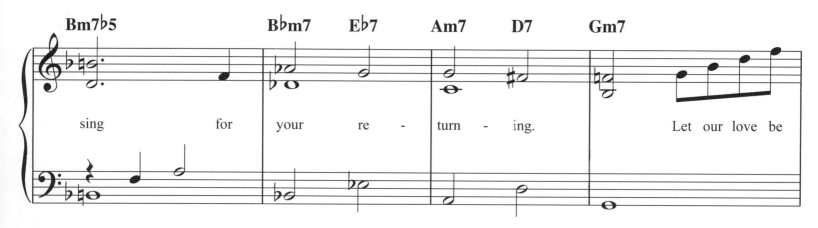

sing   for   your   re   -   turn   -   ing.   Let our love be

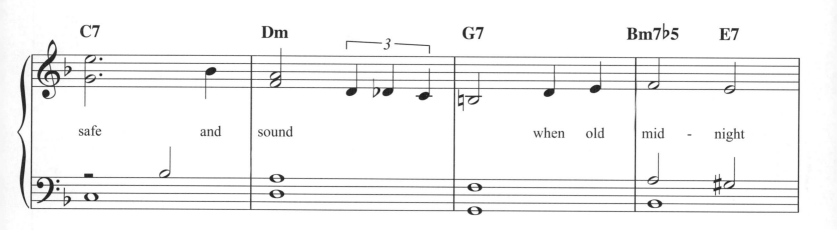

safe   and   sound   when old   mid - night

comes   a -   round. _____

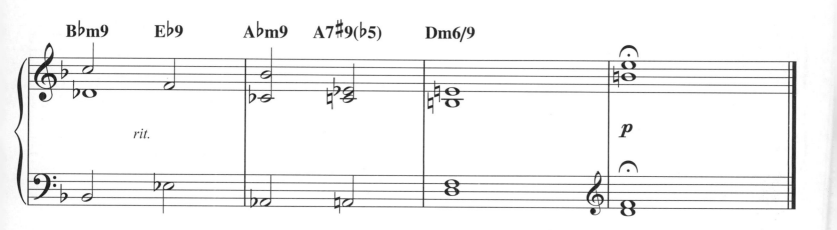

rit.   *p*

SOFTLY AS IN A MORNING SUNRISE
from THE NEW MOON

Lyrics by OSCAR HAMMERSTEIN II
Music by SIGMUND ROMBERG

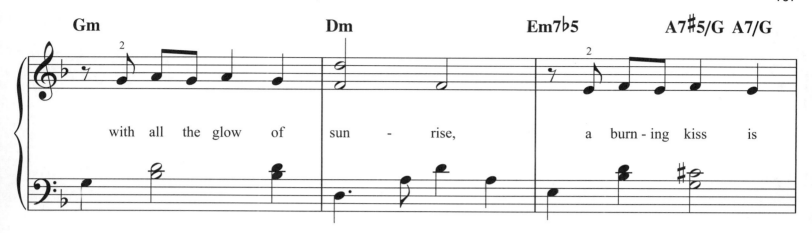

with all the glow of sun - rise, a burn - ing kiss is

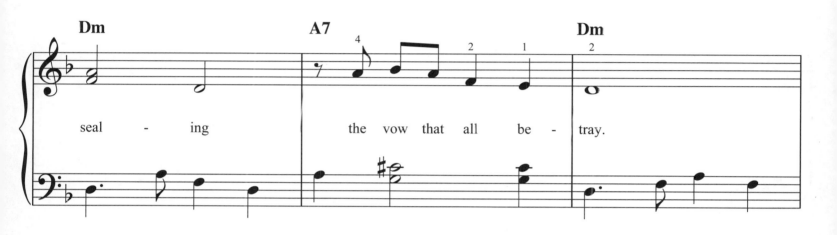

seal - ing the vow that all be - tray.

For the pas - sions that thrill love and lift you high to

heav - en are the pas - sions that kill love

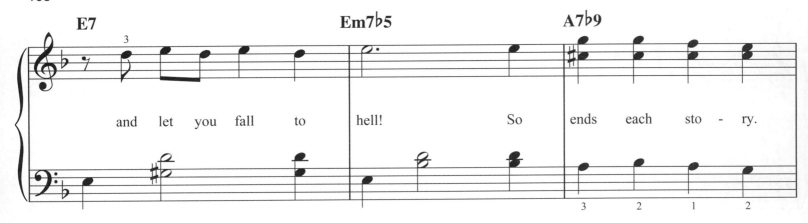

E7   **Em7♭5**   **A7♭9**

and let you fall to hell! So ends each sto - ry.

Dm   **Gm**   **Dm**

Soft - ly   as in an eve - ning sun - set,

Em7♭5   **A7♯5/G**   **A7/G**   **Dm**   **A7**

the light that gave you glo - ry will take it all a -

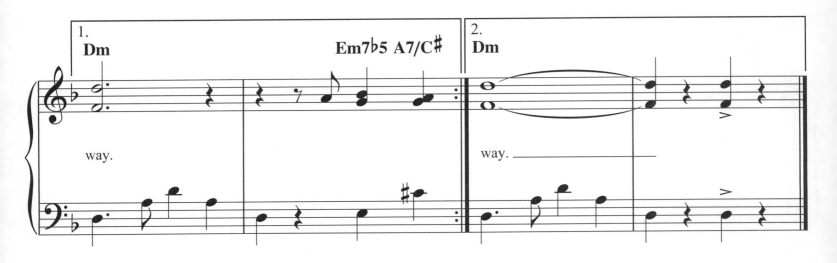

1.
Dm   **Em7♭5**   **A7/C♯**   2. **Dm**

way.   way. ____

THE SONG IS YOU

from MUSIC IN THE AIR

Lyrics by OSCAR HAMMERSTEIN II
Music by JEROME KERN

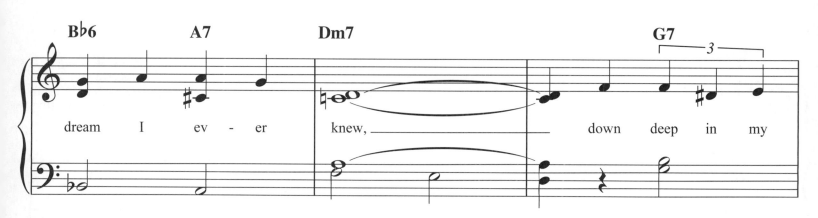

110

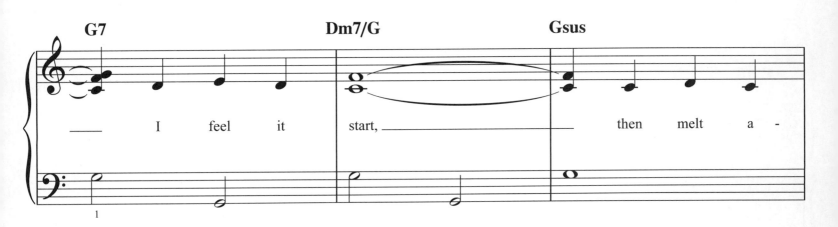

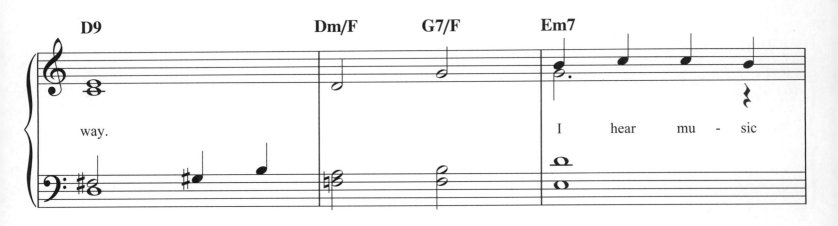

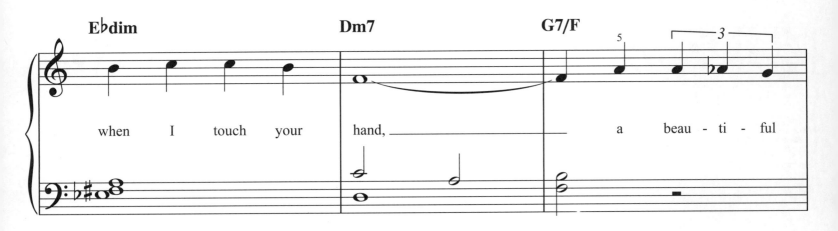

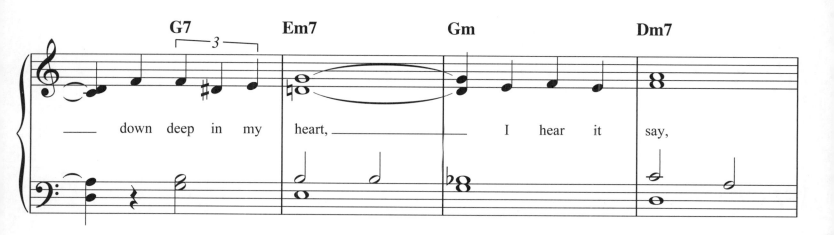

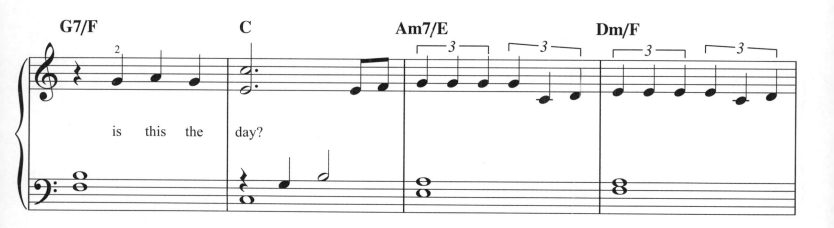

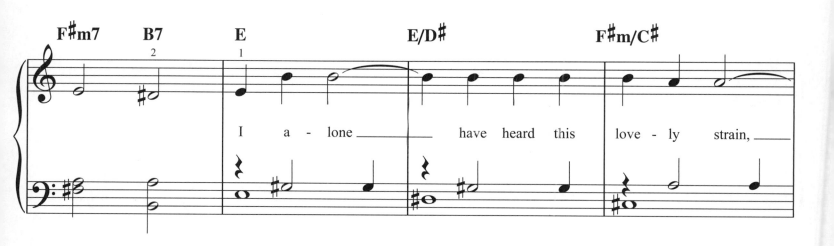

112

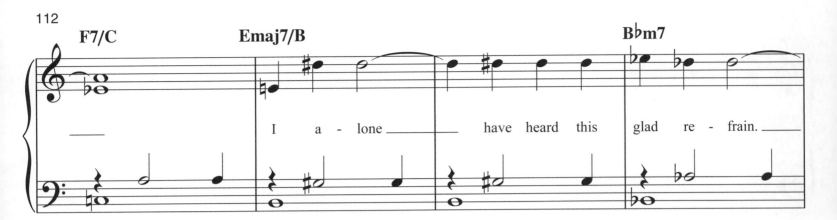

I a - lone _____ have heard this glad re - frain. _____

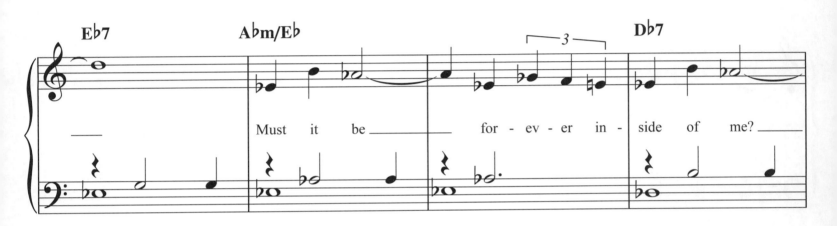

Must it be _____ for - ev - er in - side of me? _____

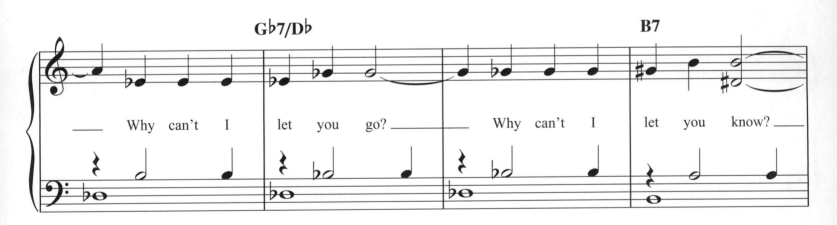

_____ Why can't I let you go? _____ Why can't I let you know? _____

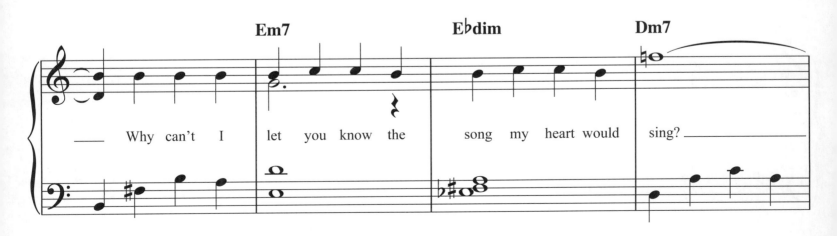

_____ Why can't I let you know the song my heart would sing? _____

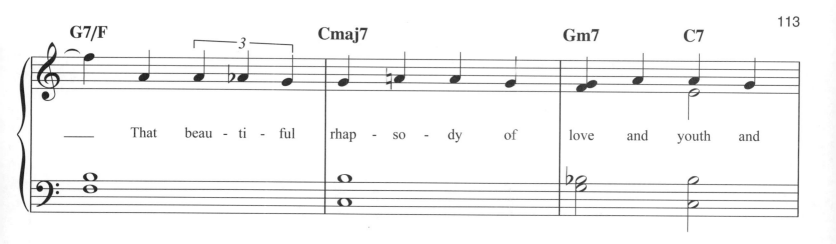

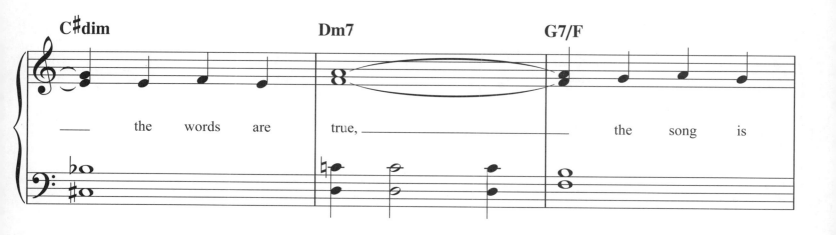

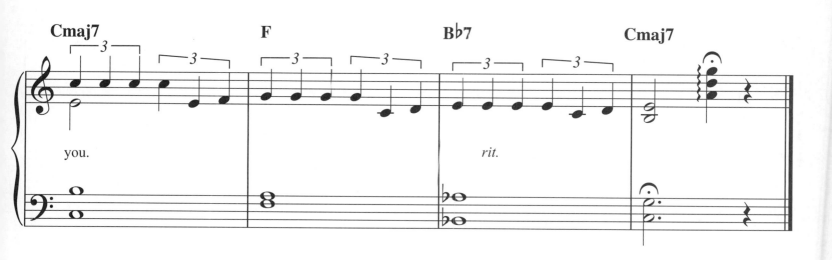

SPEAK LOW

from the Musical Production ONE TOUCH OF VENUS

Words by OGDEN NASH
Music by KURT WEILL

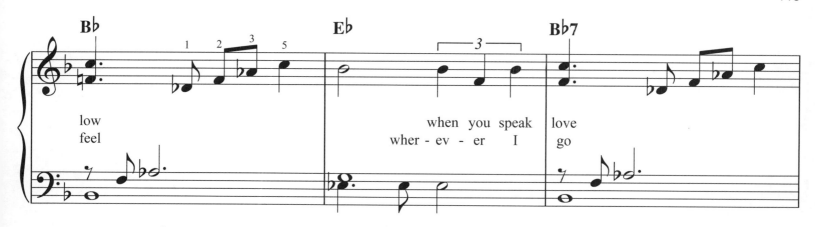

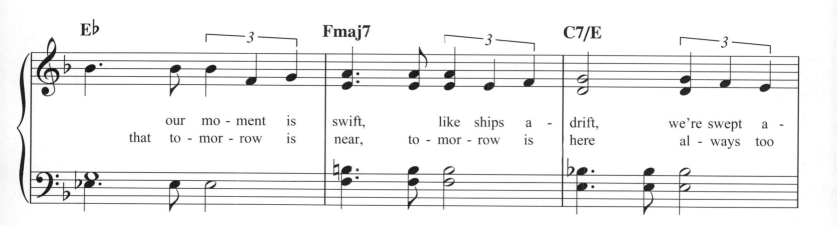

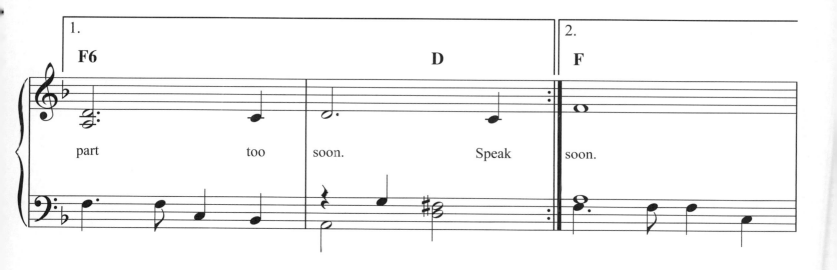

love   so   brief,   love is pure gold _____

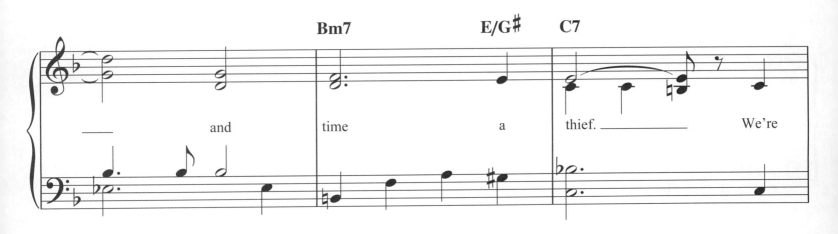

_____   and   time   a   thief. _____ We're

late,   dar - ling, we're late,

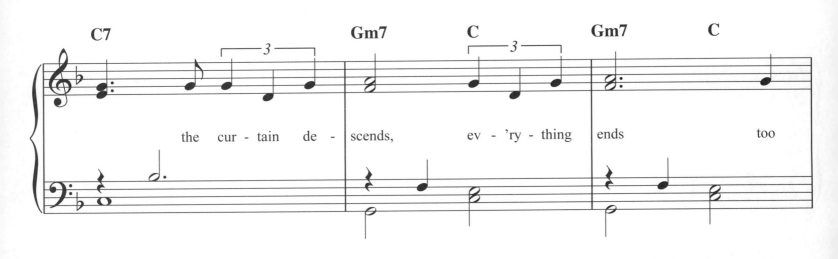

the cur - tain de - scends,   ev - 'ry - thing ends   too

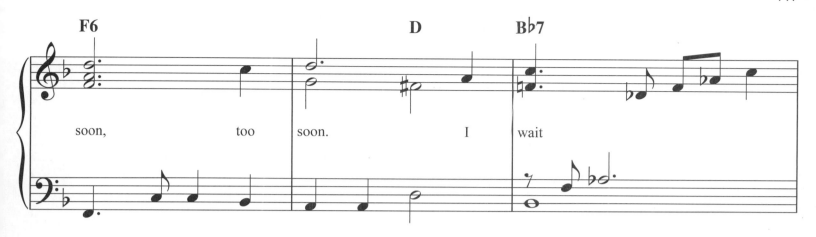

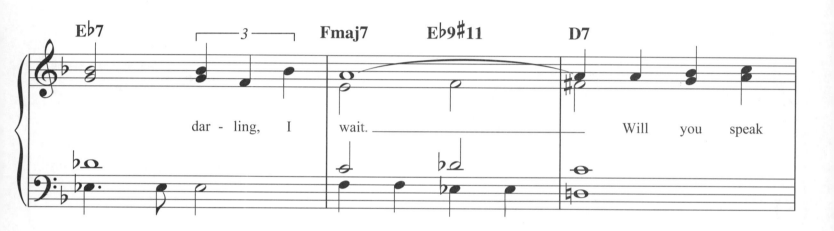

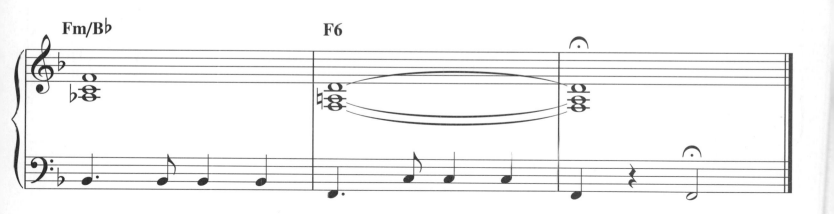

STAR EYES

Words by DON RAYE
Music by GENE DePAUL

120

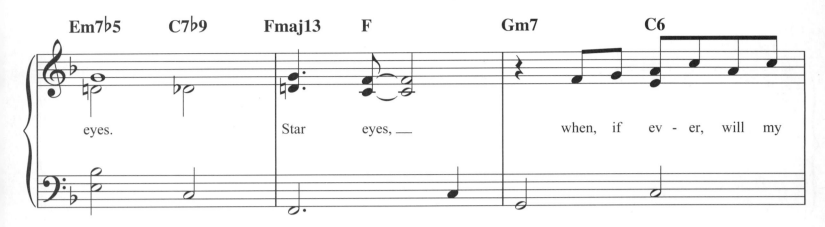

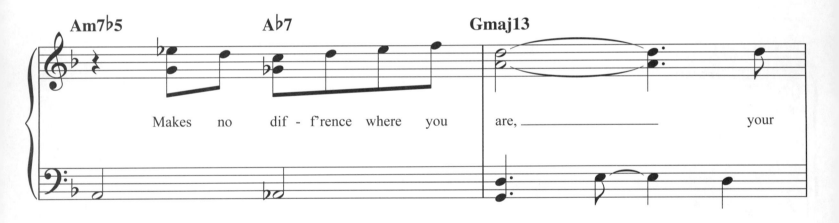

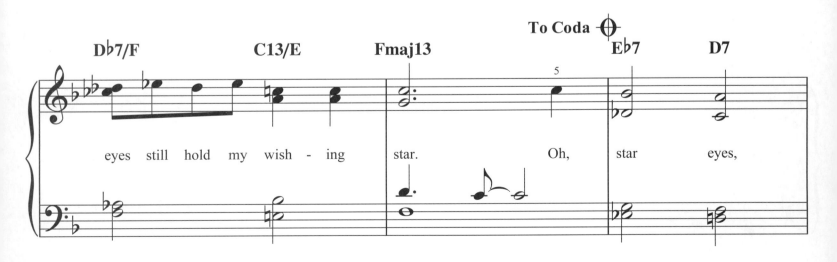

D.S. al Coda

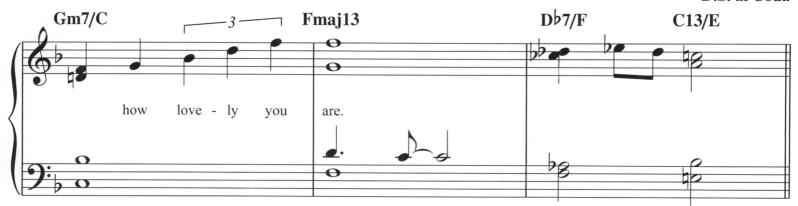

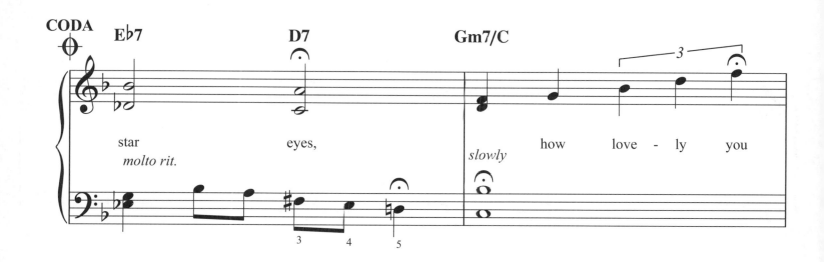

STARDUST

Words by MITCHELL PARISH
Music by HOAGY CARMICHAEL

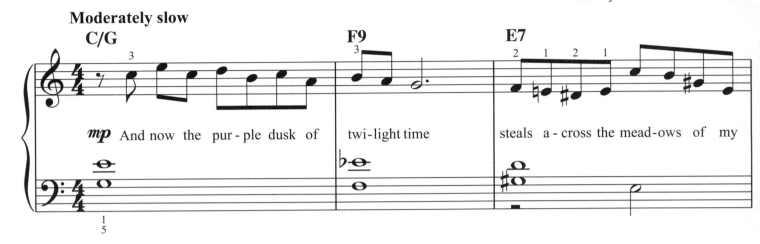

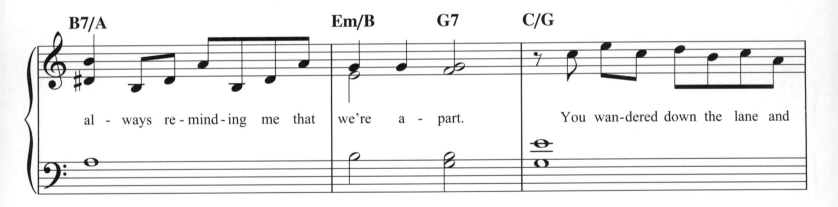

123

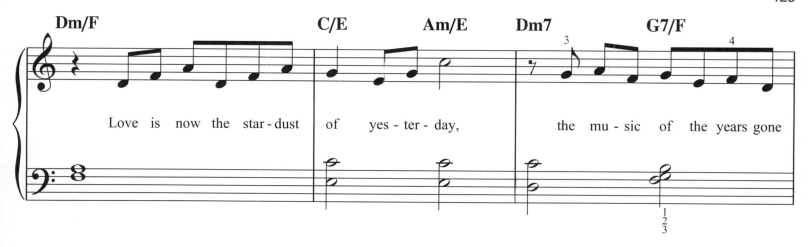

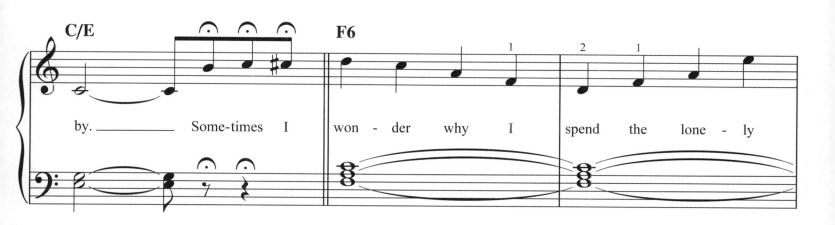

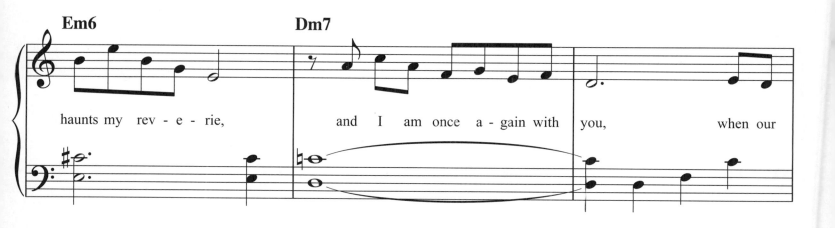

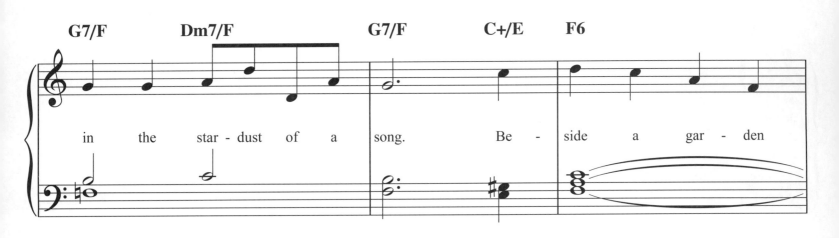

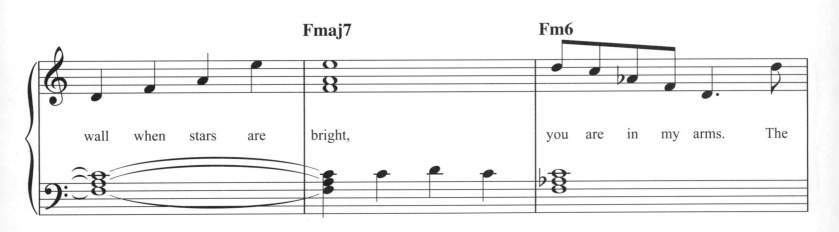

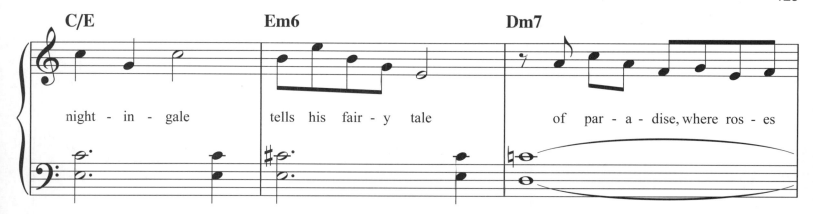

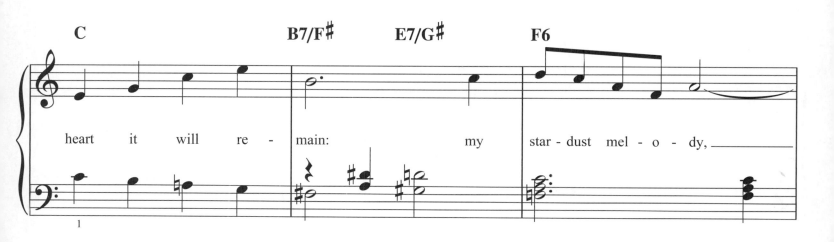

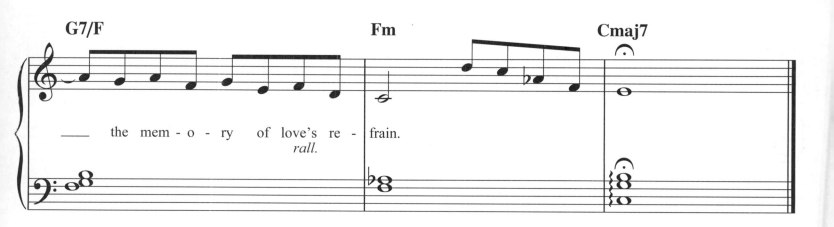

STELLA BY STARLIGHT

from the Paramount Picture THE UNINVITED

Words by NED WASHINGTON
Music by VICTOR YOUNG

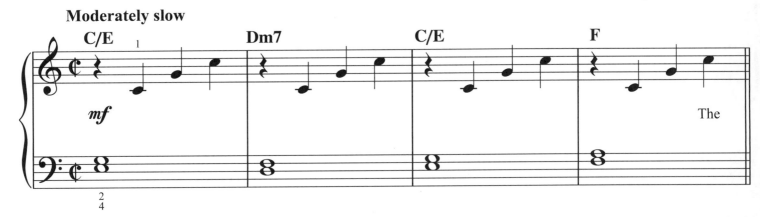

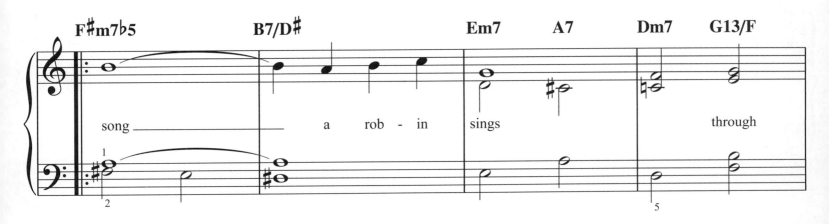

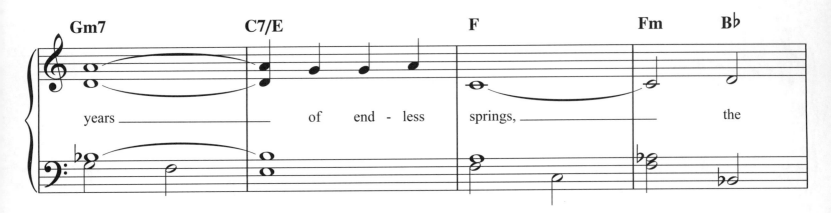

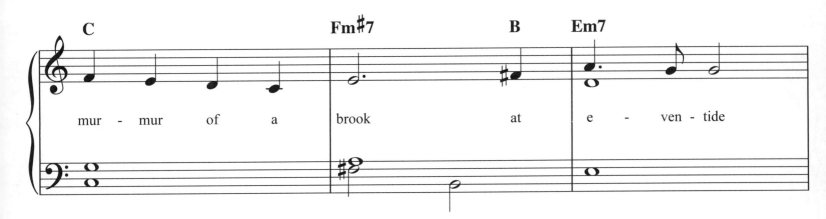

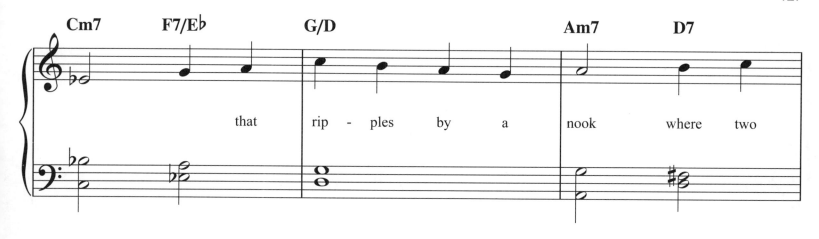

Cm7   F7/E♭   G/D   Am7   D7

that rip - ples by a nook where two

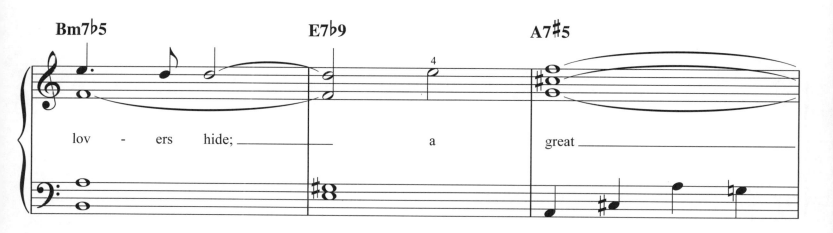

Bm7♭5   E7♭9   A7♯5

lov - ers hide; _____ a great _____

Dm7

_____ sym - phon - ic theme, _____ that's Stel - la by

Fm   C6/E

star - light _____ and not a dream. _____

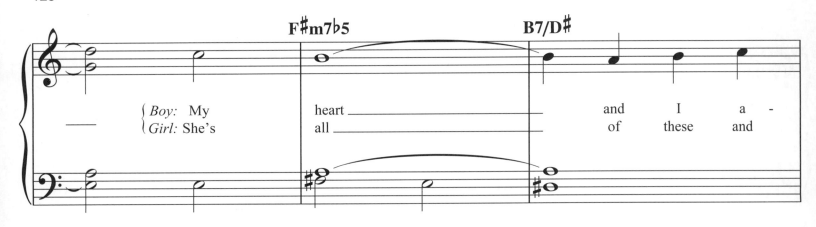

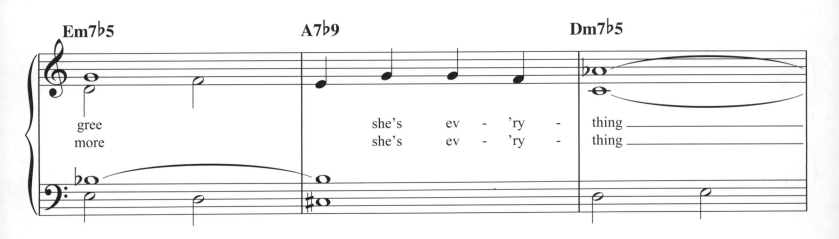

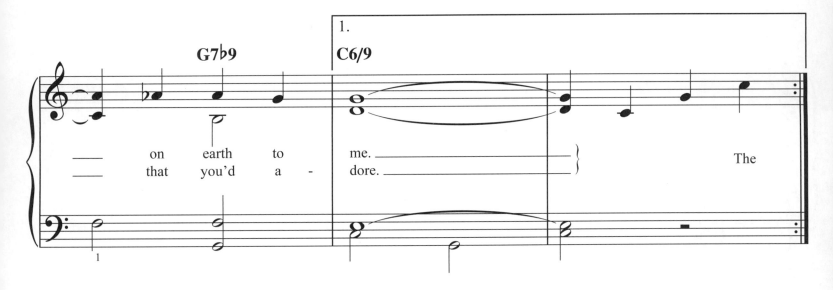

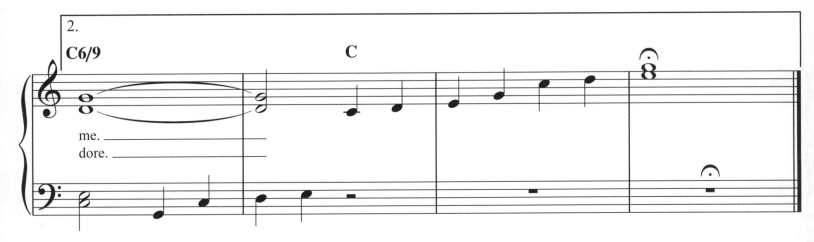

SUMMERTIME
from PORGY AND BESS®

Music and Lyrics by GEORGE GERSHWIN,
DuBOSE and DOROTHY HEYWARD
and IRA GERSHWIN

130

look - in',   so   hush, lit - tle ba - by,   don' __   you

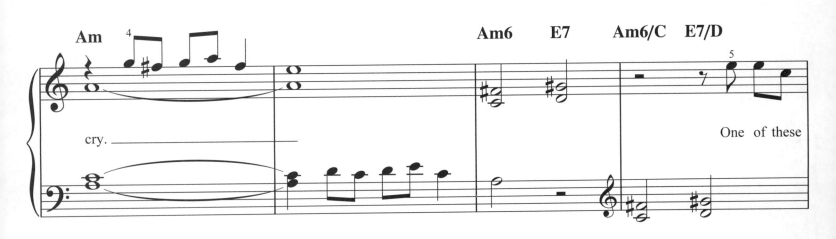

cry. _____   One of these

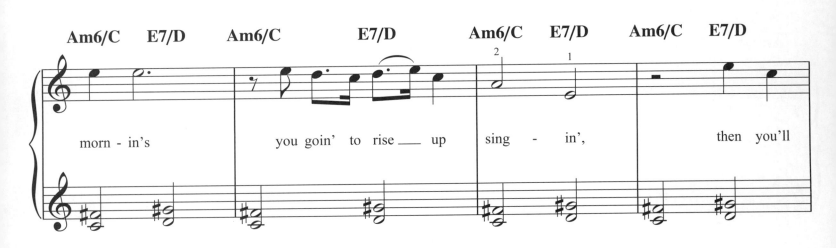

morn - in's   you goin' to rise __ up   sing - in',   then you'll

spread   yo'   wings   an' you'll take ____ the   sky. _____

131

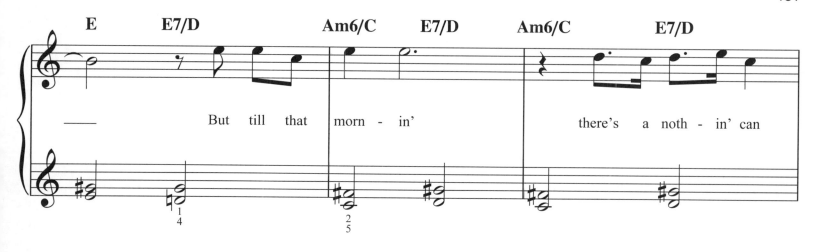

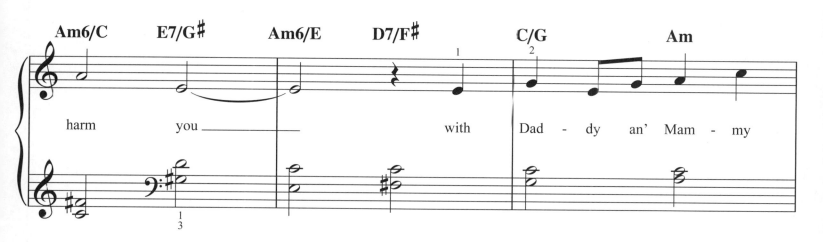

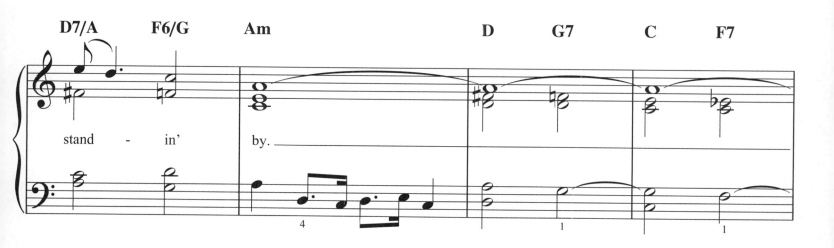

TANGERINE
from the Paramount Picture THE FLEET'S IN

Words by JOHNNY MERCER
Music by VICTOR SCHERTZINGER

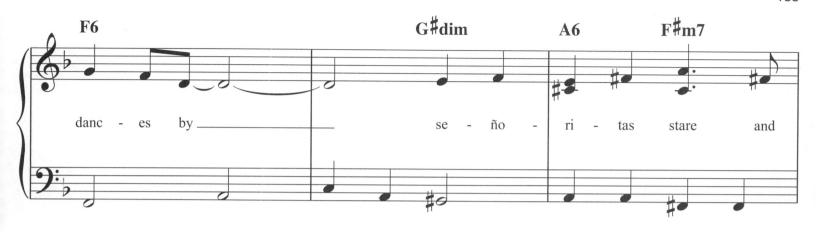

F6   G#dim   A6   F#m7

danc - es by _____ se - ño - ri - tas stare and

Bm7   E7   A   D7#5

ca - ba - lle - ros sigh.   And I've

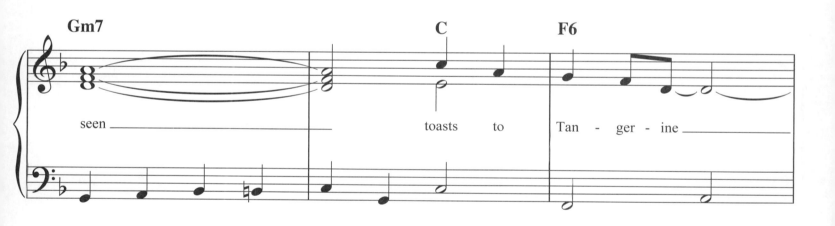

Gm7   C   F6

seen _____ toasts to Tan - ger - ine _____

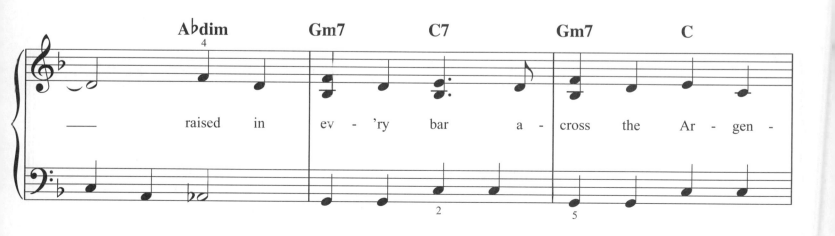

A♭dim   Gm7   C7   Gm7   C

____ raised in ev - 'ry bar a - cross the Ar - gen -

134

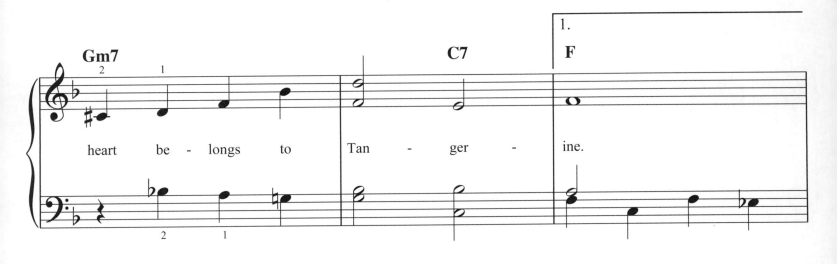

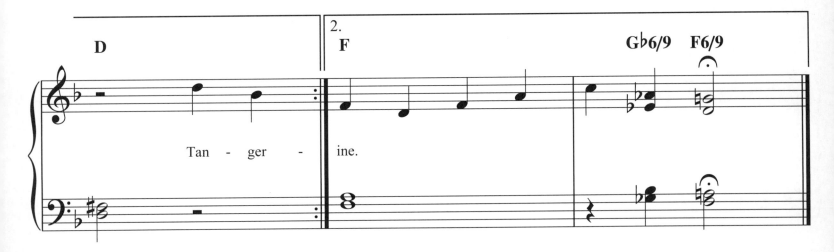

THERE IS NO GREATER LOVE

Words by MARTY SYMES
Music by ISHAM JONES

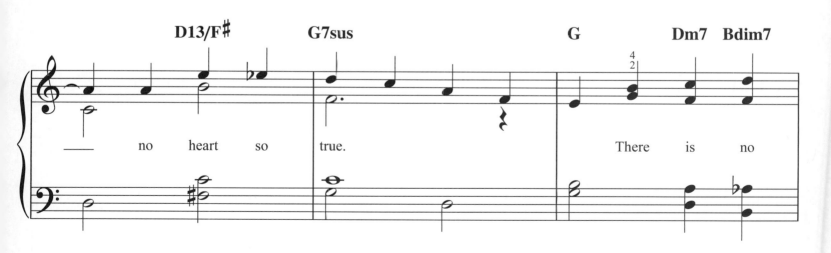

great - er thrill than | what you bring to | me, _____

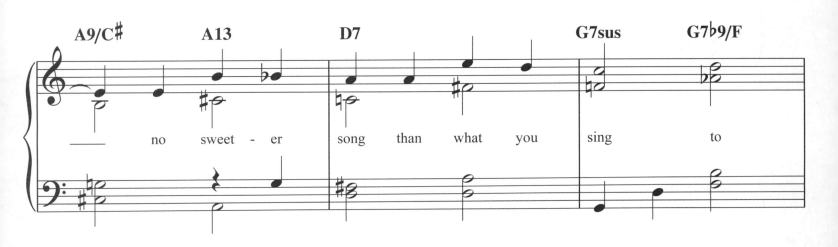

_____ no sweet - er | song than what you | sing to

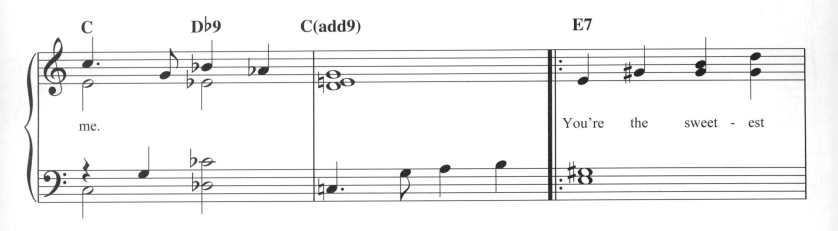

me. | | You're the sweet - est

thing | I have ev - er known,

and to think that you are mine a - lone!

There is no great - er love in all the world, it's

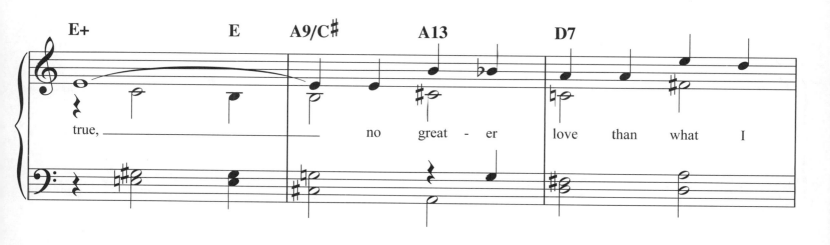

true, _____ no great - er love than what I

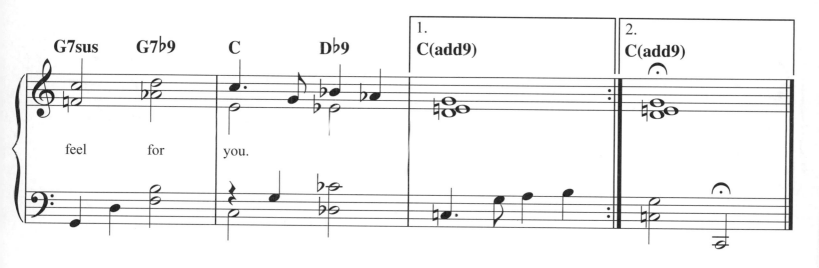

feel for you.

TENDERLY
from TORCH SONG

Lyric by JACK LAWRENCE
Music by WALTER GROSS

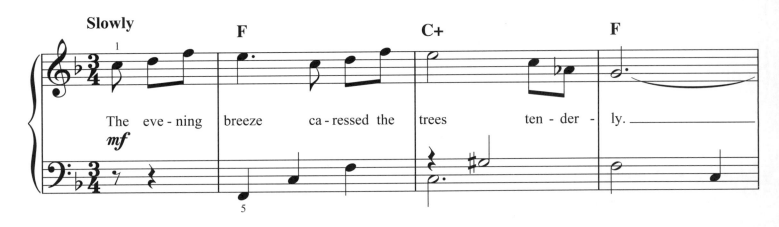

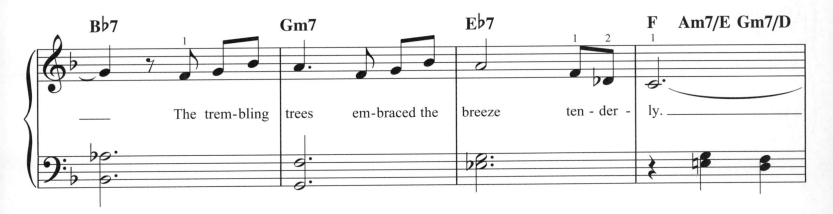

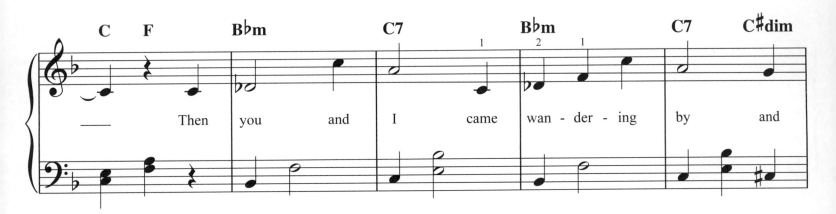

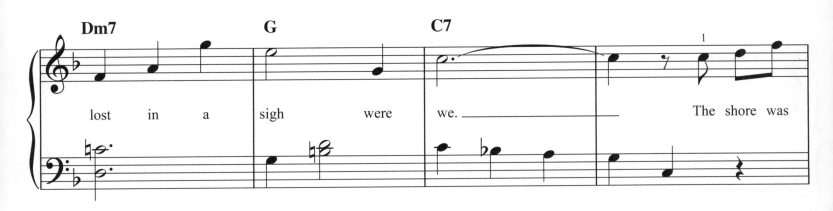

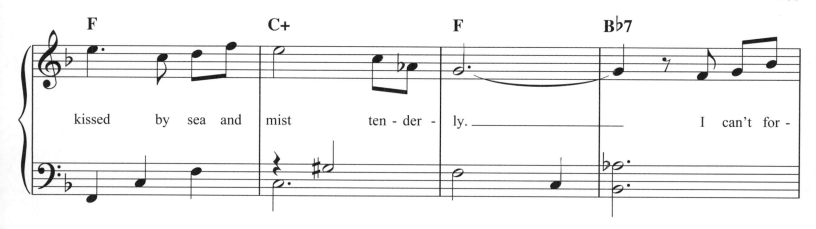

kissed by sea and mist ten - der - ly. _____ I can't for -

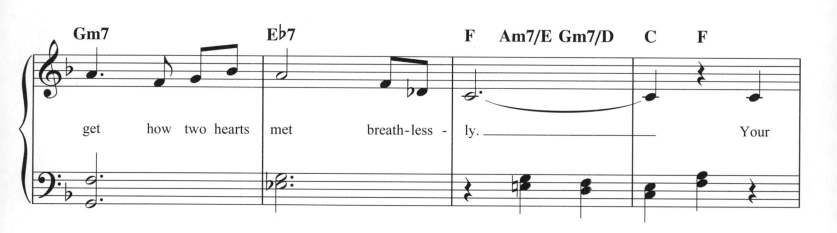

get how two hearts met breath-less - ly. _____ Your

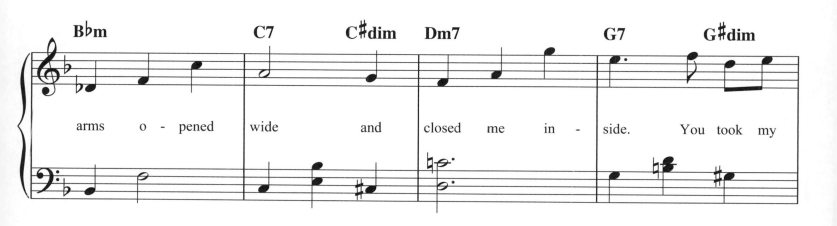

arms o - pened wide and closed me in - side. You took my

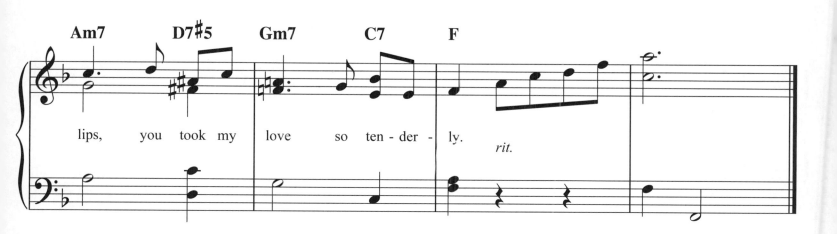

lips, you took my love so ten - der - ly. *rit.*

THERE WILL NEVER BE ANOTHER YOU

from the Motion Picture ICELAND

Lyric by MACK GORDON
Music by HARRY WARREN

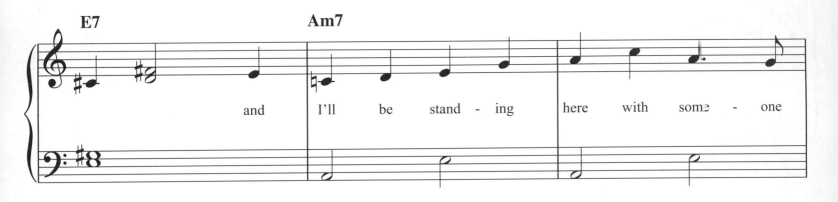

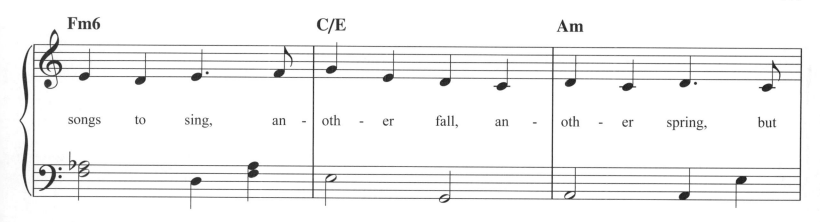

songs to sing, an - oth - er fall, an - oth - er spring, but

there will nev - er be an - oth - er you.

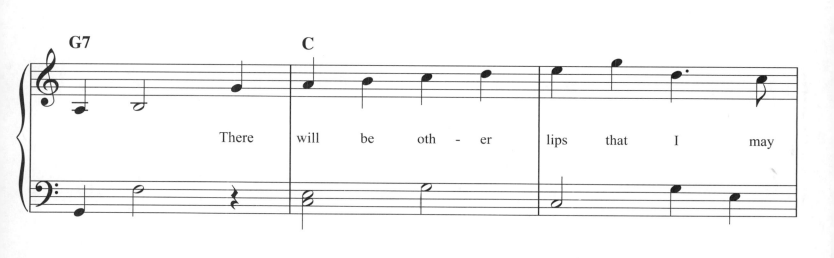

There will be oth - er lips that I may

kiss, but they won't thrill me

like   yours   used   to   do.   Yes,

I   may   dream   a   mil - lion   dreams,   but   how   can   they   come

true,   if   there   will   nev - er   ev - er   be   an -

oth - er   you?   There   you?

WHEN I FALL IN LOVE
from ONE MINUTE TO ZERO

Words by EDWARD HEYMAN
Music by VICTOR YOUNG

Moderately slow

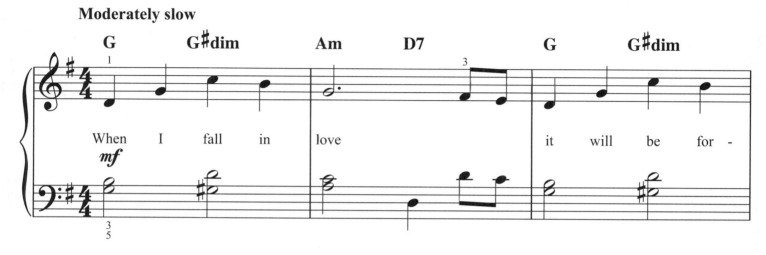

When I fall in love it will be for -

ev - er, or I'll nev - er fall in

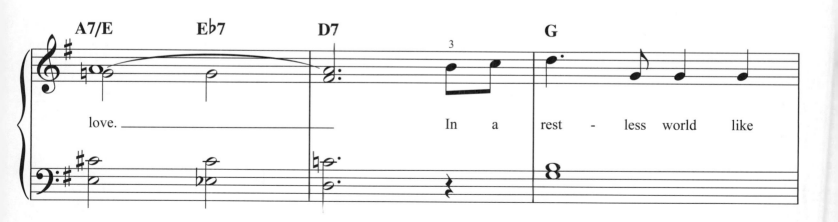

love. _____ In a rest - less world like

this is,   love is   end - ed be - fore it's be gun,   and too

man - y moon - light   kiss - es   seem to   cool in the warmth of the

rit.

sun.   When I give my   heart

a tempo

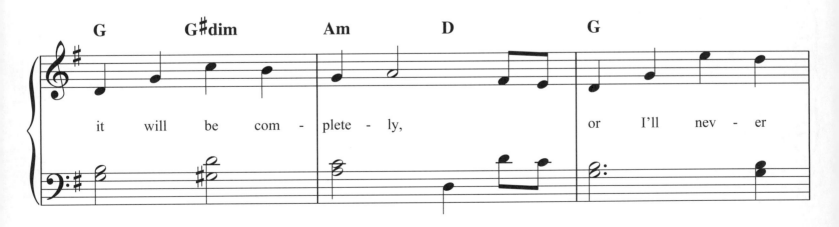

it will be com - plete - ly,   or I'll nev - er

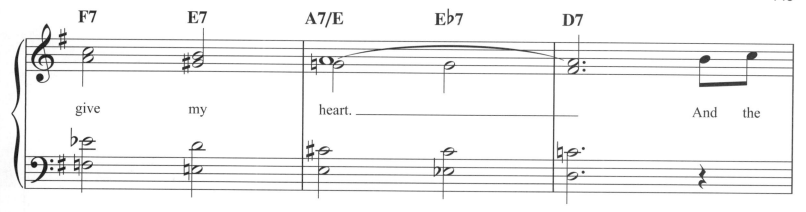

give my   my   heart. _____   And   the

mo - ment I can   feel   that   you   feel   that   way

too   is   when   I   fall   in   love   with

rit.   *a tempo*

you.   you.

rit.

The Way You Look Tonight

from SWING TIME

Words by DOROTHY FIELDS
Music by JEROME KERN

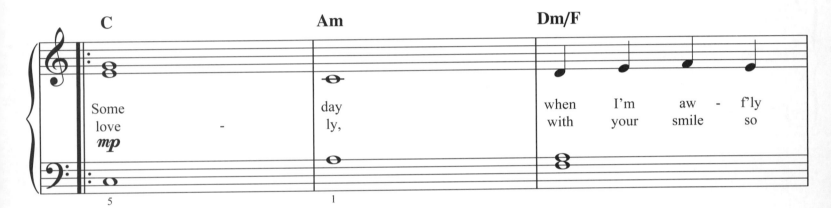

you
you

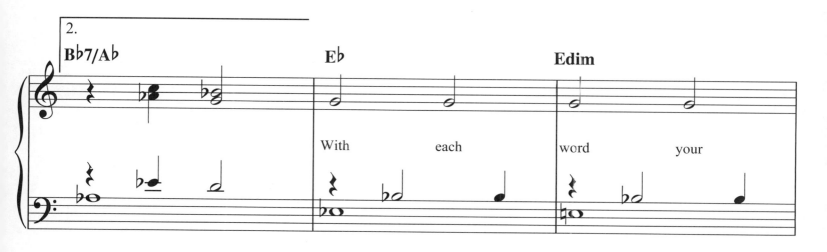

night. · · and the way you look to -
night. · · just the the way you look to -

1.
Oh, but you're

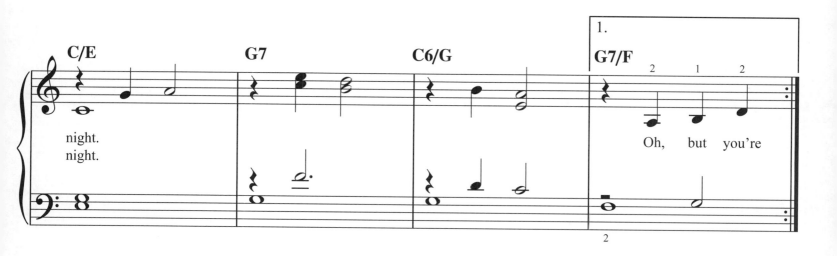

2.
With each word your

ten - der - ness grows, · · tear - ing my fear

F#dim — Fm7 — Bb7 — Eb

a - part. And that

Edim7 — Fm7 — Bb7/Ab — Eb/G

laugh that wrin - kles your nose touch - es my

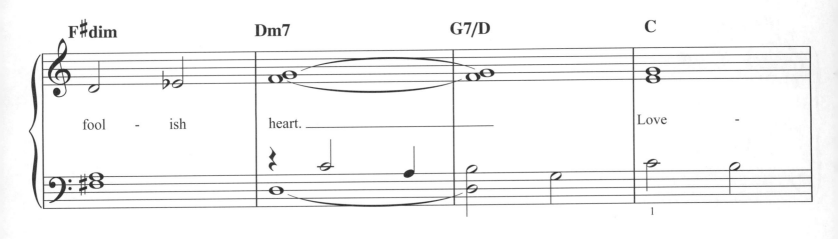

F#dim — Dm7 — G7/D — C

fool - ish heart. Love -

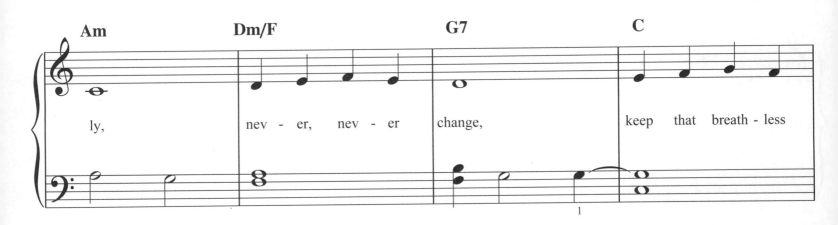

Am — Dm/F — G7 — C

ly, nev - er, nev - er change, keep that breath - less

C#dim7 **Dm7** **G7/D**

charm. Won't you please ar - range it, 'cause I

Gm7 **C7/E** **F6** **G7**

love you, just the way you look to -

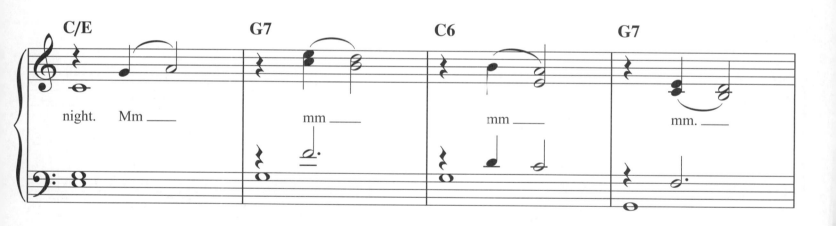

C/E **G7** **C6** **G7**

night. Mm ____ mm ____ mm ____ mm. ____

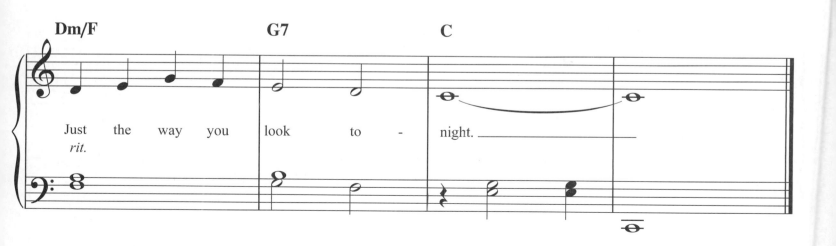

Dm/F **G7** **C**

Just the way you look to - night. ____
rit.

YOU BROUGHT A NEW KIND OF LOVE TO ME

from the Paramount Picture THE BIG POND

Words and Music by SAMMY FAIN,
IRVING KAHAL and PIERRE NORMAN

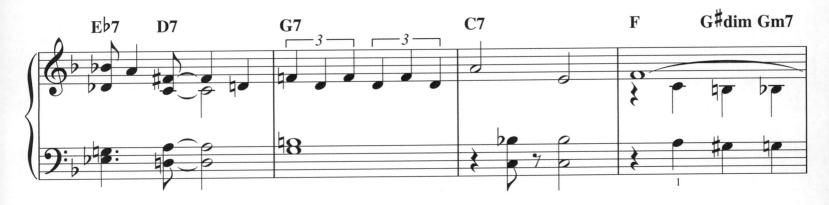

Sweet one, ___ fair - er than the flow - ers, ___

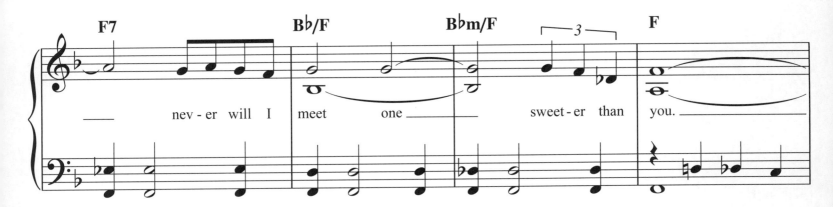

___ nev - er will I meet one ___ sweet - er than you.

Would you _____ turn a - way or could you _____

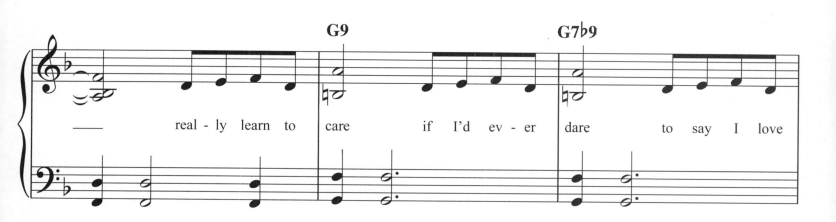

_____ real - ly learn to care if I'd ev - er dare to say I love

you? _____ If the night - in - gales ___ could

sand - man brought __ me

sing like you ___ they'd sing much sweet - er than they do _____ for

dreams of you ___ I'd want to sleep my whole life through, _ for

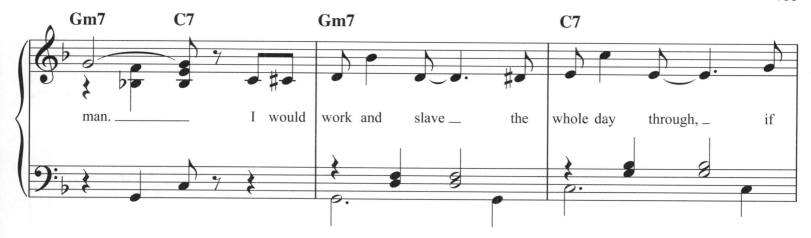

Gm7   C7   Gm7   C7

man. _____ I would work and slave _ the whole day through, _ if

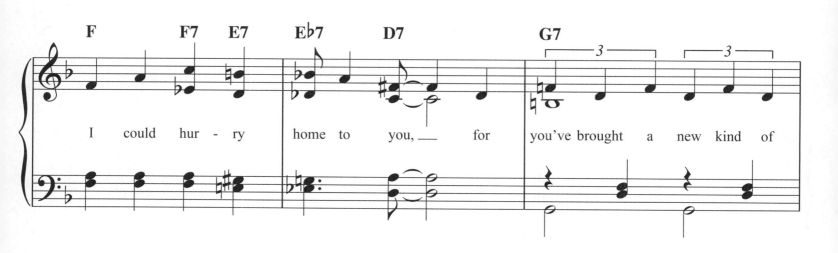

F   F7   E7   E♭7   D7   G7

I could hur - ry home to you, _ for you've brought a new kind of

C7   C/B♭   Am7♭5   D   G7

love to me. You've brought a new kind of

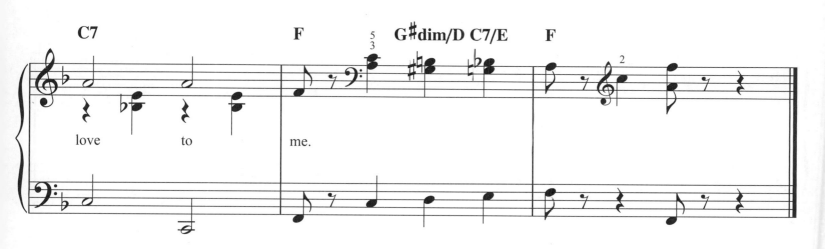

C7   F   G♯dim/D   C7/E   F

love to me.

YOU STEPPED OUT OF A DREAM

Words by GUS KAHN
Music by NACIO HERB BROWN

Tempo I (♩♩ = ♩♪)

You ____ stepped out of a dream,

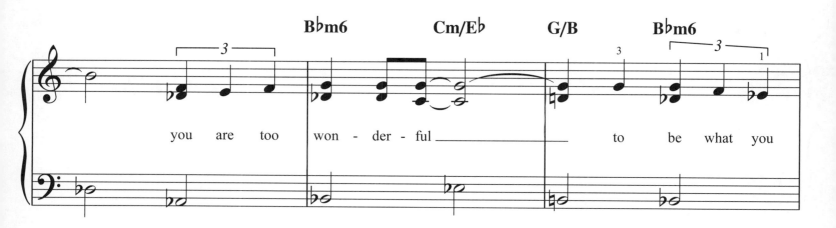

you are too won - der - ful _____ to be what you

seem. ____ Could there be eyes like yours, _____

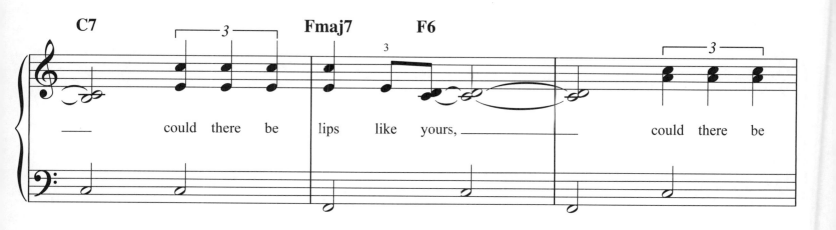

____ could there be lips like yours, _____ could there be

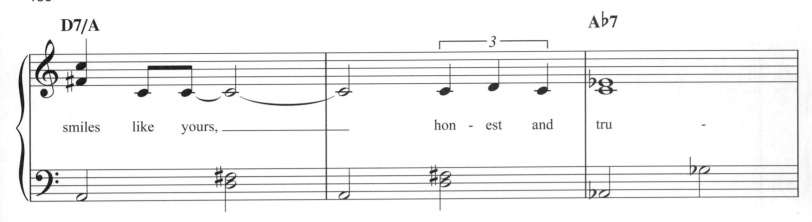

smiles like yours, _____ hon - est and tru -

ly? You stepped out of a

cloud. I want to take you a - way, _____

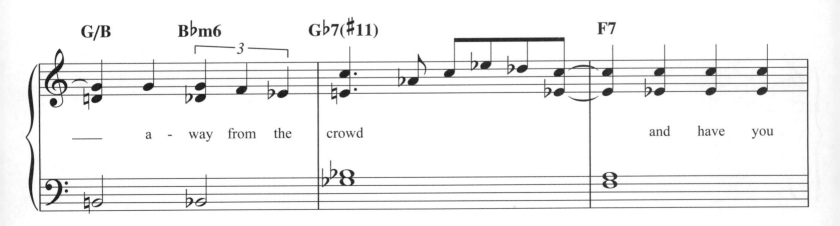

____ a - way from the crowd and have you

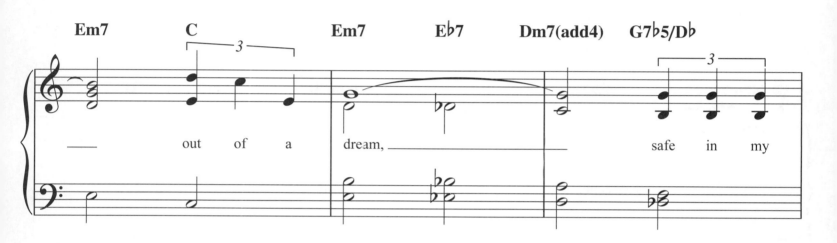

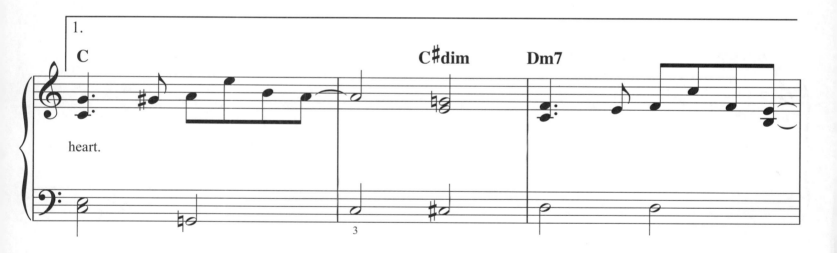

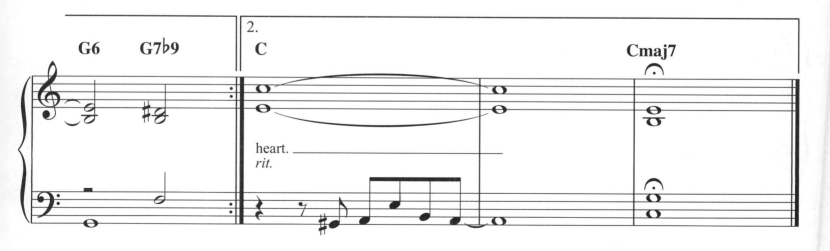

WHEN SUNNY GETS BLUE

Lyrics by JACK SEGAL
Music by MARVIN FISHER

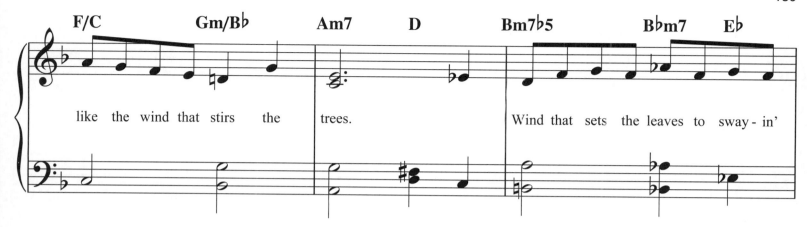

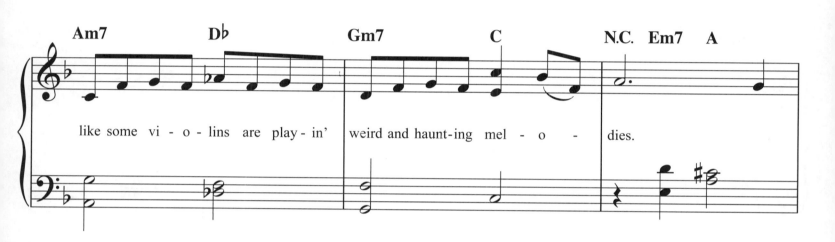

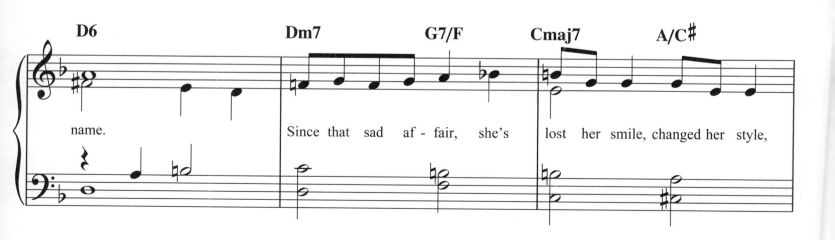

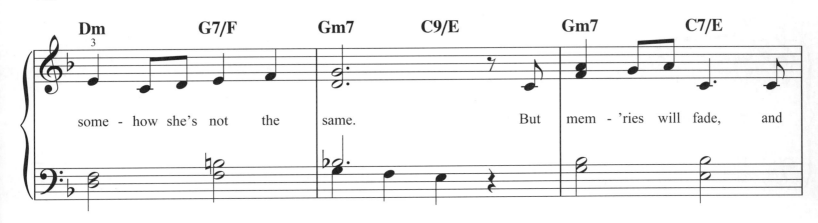

some - how she's not the same. But mem - 'ries will fade, and

pret - ty dreams will rise up where her oth - er dream fell through.

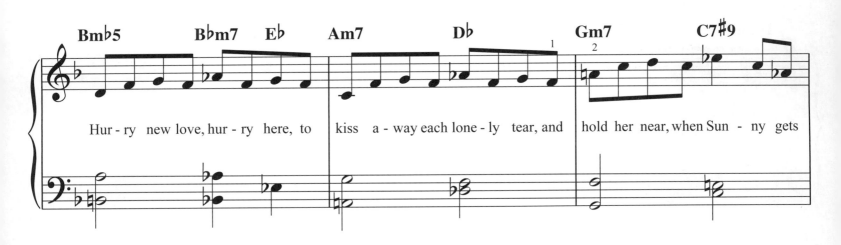

Hur - ry new love, hur - ry here, to kiss a - way each lone - ly tear, and hold her near, when Sun - ny gets

blue. Hold her near, when Sun - ny gets blue.